YOU
ARE A RACIST!!!!

YOU
ARE A RACIST!!!!

And other works

MYRON CHERRY

Relax—Everybody is a racist—it's NATURAL !!
It's a Basic Survival Mechanism.

Here's the fundamental law:
 **"ALL SENTIENT CREATURES ARE MOST
COMFORTABLE WITH THEIR OWN KIND."**

authorHOUSE®

AuthorHouse™
1663 Liberty Drive
Bloomington, IN 47403
www.authorhouse.com
Phone: 1-800-839-8640

First published by AuthorHouse   09/16/2011

ISBN: 978-1-4634-2442-8 (sc)
ISBN: 978-1-4634-2443-5 (hc)
ISBN: 978-1-4634-2444-2 (ebk)

Library of Congress Control Number: 2011911128

Printed in the United States of America

Contents

Preface

This book is not so much well-researched as it is well-remembered. There are no footnotes or references. Much of it is autobiographical in origin, being both observed and experienced. Not all events seemed to require a conclusion at the time; they were simply experienced and observed; but looking back, one can form a conclusion today and see a larger, longer picture. One of the blessing/curse aspects of a long life is that some things are remembered differently than they were recorded by the media. Revisionist history often starts with slanted contemporary reporting which may poison or sweeten the record that others will follow and depend upon.

The author remembers the 'Great Depression' as an active time; people might not have much money, but they kept busy, made the best of it, and found entertaining things to do. (Entertainment seems to be a human drive, as much as survival itself, not as intense but continuous.) Schools had ball games, musicals, plays, and other events, holidays came and went, people died and babies were born. There were great moments and sad ones. Life goes on.

Events today are critical and fast moving, we are told. They appear to be more exciting, but there are gaps. Some factors are given great importance while others get little attention. During the 'O.J. Trial' it seemed nothing else was happening. But there was another trial going on, in Federal Court in Texas. The Branch Davidian survivors were being tried for some federal offense in Waco (?) Texas. One of the defendants was six months old. We couldn't find out anything, even when we asked. Our TV station said they only could show what 'came down on the feed.' Whoever controls the 'feed,' determines what events we learn about. How often does this happen ? What is happening behind the 'news' that might be important to us ? Are we only getting censored news ? Are we being fed the true story or only the 'approved' version ? Who approves it ?

When we see TV reporters fixated on a little girl's death in Florida, we wonder – is something important being covered up ?

All Sentient Creatures Are Most Comfortable With Their Own Kind

This fundamental law is so obvious that it has been overlooked by behaviorist commentators and the general public.

The Corollary to this law is "It is normal for all sentient creatures to be suspicious of others who are different from themselves."

When a sentient creature is first born, it seeks comfort and avoids discomfort. Typically, the mother offers comfort and establishes rapport for that particular species. The sentient creature recognizes its mother's (and its own) species as being safe and comfortable. From then on, others will be judged by comparison with that first impression. When meeting new entities the sentient creature will compare and evaluate them based on its own past experience. The sentient creature will prefer the company of entities like its mother and itself. Others will have to 'prove themselves.'

With experience, the sentient creature will find that entities different than its mother seldom offer the same comfort, and are therefore less appealing. The choice soon becomes; similar for comfort versus different. Different is to be avoided or at least ignored. The personality has been set: Similarity is good. Different is suspect.

As the creature grows and gains more experience, it expands its ability to evaluate other entities, and will modify its original simplistic criteria, but the basic comparison is always in the background.

The foregoing applies to all sentient creatures, not just humans. However, as they develop, human babies become more discerning about things they observe, and they will question what they perceive. Even without the vocabulary and verbal skills, the baby's life is 'notice and compare,' 'notice and compare,' 'notice and compare.' Lower species do not question, they accept 'what is.'

The human baby will notice and compare its similarity with other humans around it. One of the obvious comparisons will be skin color. The old comparison is still there; Similarity is good; different is suspect and raises the question 'why?'

If the baby's skin color is the same as all those around it, there is no question. If the baby had fur and all those around it had fur, there would be no question. If the baby's skin color is different from those around it, there is the question 'why?' and 'do I belong here?' And also 'What am I?' A question has been raised that may haunt it for the rest of its life if there is a difference.

Skin color is very obvious to the sentient creature, and the sentient creature has a strong desire to be a comfortable part of the surrounding world. Popularity polls show that more than 90% of blacks (and browns) support President Obama for reelection. Is that racist? Of course. It's natural. He's family.

The baby will follow 'notice and compare' with 'notice, compare, and imitate.' By imitating, it will be conforming to those around it. It will imitate within its abilities to do so.

Conformity is an urge, just as much as other urges. To conform brings comfort, approval, and security. Even 'non-conformists' are imitating someone they admire. 'George Washington was a rebel, so if I rebel, I am like George Washington.' Or 'the rock star xyz has his nose pierced, so if I have my nose pierced, I am like him. It's often humorous to observe a group of 'non-conformists' because they are so similar in their appearance. The baby wants to conform, so as to be secure and comfortable.

Guilt, however, is an external mechanism by which others try to exploit differences and questions to their own advantage or profit. They would infer that reacting to differences with suspicion is somehow wrong. Ironically, they would replace someone else's individual preference with their own (self serving) preference. Those exploiters of differences presume their own preferences are morally superior to all others, and they insist that others must change. Those exploiters are racists themselves because they are discriminating against others who are different from themselves.

Anytime such an attitude or belief is accepted by some as undeniable truth, it is worth examining in an objective, unbiased way. So it is when guilt is associated with racial differences. If behavior inherently natural to the species is misinterpreted as something unnatural to be corrected, we should analyze to see if the correction is worse than the supposed character flaw, or if there is any character flaw at all. The character flaw may be in those casting aspersions of racism.

Today, many individuals and organizations operate successfully and profitably by using racial 'guilt' as their theme, to the exclusion of rational thinking. They exploit racial abuses in actions present and past, to infer that others are guilty for inequities they suffer today, real or imagined. Their Selective Rage is transparent and self serving when viewed objectively. By making unrealistic assertions, they are as racist as those they would condemn.

So what? The important point is, 'racism' is natural and there is no shame or guilt attached to it. Natural Preference is natural and nothing to be ashamed of anymore than being ashamed of having opposing thumbs. We are not guilty of something that is natural. We are all most comfortable with our own kind, and there is nothing wrong with that.

The 'Racist' Game

When black slaves were imported into the South to work on the plantations, they *were* inferior, coming from a stone age, tribal society into a literate, relatively advanced and complicated society. But they learned, and their children learned, and their grandchildren learned. Another faction soon noticed and seized upon the situation; Northern Christians. Unlike many other religions, Christians have a sympathy for the less fortunate, and the black slaves in the South were obviously less free than any others in the United States, where freedom was the measure of a government and enshrined in the Constitution. There was soon a Colloquial Attitude, aided by popular writings, that *all* slaves were mistreated and lived lives of misery. Most Northerners became sympathetic to black people, even if they had never seen one. It is likely that many slaves were treated well, at least physically. As property, it would be in the owners best interest to keep them in good health and relatively happy.

Slaves were an investment for them, much like horses and farm equipment. You protect your investments.

The stereotype persisted however, and even led to our Civil War. After the war, there were attempts to 'right' the 'wrongs' of the past by law. But law is always a poor mechanism to change something as complicated as human nature. Laws typically have unintended consequences, and even more so in emotionally charged issues, where the 'cure' will likely excel in the opposite direction. Federal bureaucrats in that aftermath of the Civil War were as clumsy and inept as bureaucrats are today.

'Discrimination' used to be a flattering word. "The discriminating user will appreciate the superiority of our product." Today, 'discrimination' and a new word 'dissing' (for disrespecting) are tokens for alleged mistreatment, usually of a racist nature. (This is another example of a group appropriating a word and changing its meaning for their own use.)

Opportunists are always available to take advantage of a situation, especially if they can make money from it. The Racist Game is to take the oppression of black slaves hundreds of years ago and use it to create guilt today on the part of any entity with money and power. Some opportunists can find more recent examples of 'discrimination' and create guilt out of that too. Of course, the opportunists expect to be amply rewarded financially for their altruism.

The many organizations playing the Racist Game range from blatant extortion to the sophisticated altruistic. Key to their success are sycophants in the news media, pun-dunces (pundits) who can laud their successes and ignore their blatant excesses. Uniformity of opinion, supplied by a sympathetic (echo-chamber) news media, can enhance the appearance of righteousness posed by practitioners of the Racist Game.

There are many blacks who are quietly successful in today's society. They have achieved that success on their own merits, without fanfare, in a competitive environment. Their successes are downplayed, ignored, and even attacked by those using the Racist Game for their own monetary objectives. We should be proud of those who can ignore race and succeed in our free-enterprise system.

Generalizations

Generalizations are efficiency mechanisms based on past experience. We learn to form generalizations and habits so that we don't have to repeat the effort to analyze every situation anew. In some instances, a generalization is a life-saving mechanism. Even a fish will learn from one encounter that a certain type of predator is a threat. Generalizations are often criticized as bad, but they lead to time-saving habits. Indeed, it can be said that our lives are governed and simplified by habits learned from generalizations. It's as if we teach our subconscious how to do something, which when learned, can free us to think about other things. Once we learn to ride a bicycle, our subconscious can do that task and take it over, so we can direct our attention to other things.

Generalizations about race and ethnicity are common. Generalizations based on past observations lead quickly to Stereotypes. Even without personal experience, the opinions of others can lead to stereotypes, such as "Pit-bull dogs are always vicious and threatening." Stereotypes are Generalizations personified, rightly or wrongly.

We are reminded of the statement "All generalizations are wrong, including this one." However, we all use generalizations and habits and always will. They are practical and time saving. We doubt that detractors can come up with something better.

Anecdote Exploitation

In contrast to generalizations, there is Anecdote Exploitation. An anecdote of course, is a personal story or experience, which often is unusual, contrary to general belief, or with an unusual result. Anecdote Exploitation is commonly used by some to gain sympathy, raise money. or promote a personal view that the anecdote presents.

Using an example to explain a point is acceptable, but to use an exaggeration to mislead away from the truth, is despicable and becomes Anecdote Exploitation.

Anecdote Exploitation is a popular political ploy. Politicians will pick a tragic, sad case to gain sympathy for a political objective. The sadder and more tragic they can make the situation sound, the better. The sad case may or may not exist in reality, and if exaggeration helps, they would use that too. The sad case need not be typical of the whole population, and in fact is usually atypical. It usually appears to be something that most people did not think of, but should have, and are guilty for not knowing about it. "And shame on you for not being sympathetic."

Doublespeak

Washington 'Doublespeak' is another popular political ploy. Doublespeak is an effective way of hiding the original intent. Pick a word that is the opposite of the reality and then use it as the name of the deception. There are many examples of Doublespeak in government. 'Earned income' is a category in the tax code, which in fact is not income and is not earned; it is a tax benefit or loophole for certain classes, and in most cases, a payment from the government mislabeled a refund. The term 'earned income' would imply that work was done and should be rewarded with a payment of money, when in reality it is not either. Work was not done to earn it—it is a tax gimmick and a payoff for some low achievers who just may vote for those politicians who set it up.

Definitions are important. The same word or phrase can have different meanings for different groups, and result in people 'talking past' each other. Oftentimes, whoever can define the words, wins the argument despite the logic of the opposition.

During the 'Cold War,' we had 'peaceniks' and their favorite word was 'Mir.' The Russian meaning of 'Mir' was when there was no objection to communism in the whole world. The peaceniks thought 'Mir' simply meant 'Peace' and they were outspoken in mistakenly promoting it.

Washington Doublespeak is commonly used in titles of agencies and government officials. We now have 'Tsars' heading certain departments who can dictate in the name of the President. A more appropriate term would be 'Commissar' which was the name used for similar positions in communist countries after the Tsar had been overthrown.

The IRS (Internal Revenue Service) is another government bureaucracy that many would say is not really a service for the taxpayers.

However, a 'Department of Redundancy Department' might be suitably descriptive, if such a department exists.

Crumble Factor

In the most basic economic sense, there are two kinds of people—Wasters and Producers. This is not to say either one is inherently better or worse than the other nor does it categorize any person for all time. The same person may be a Waster at one time while training to be a Producer or may change from Producer to Waster because of accident, sickness, or any number of reasons. The category is not necessarily a permanent classification, either good or bad.

Producers are easy to define. They supply the basic necessities and other needed services for the members of society. Not all Producers supply food, shelter, and clothing; many do not even draw a salary. Stay-at-home mothers, for example, produce future Producers and ready them for a future contribution to society. They would be Producers. Nurses and doctors certainly provide needed services. Technicians who work with the public providing support, are Producers. Technicians who work for the government are probably Wasters, providing support for other Wasters.

Wasters are those who receive money, services, or goods from the government. Wasters do not contribute any necessities or services to the public. We are all Wasters at times when we use without producing. Children are Wasters. They use, but are not ready to produce for others. But Wasters are not inherently bad or evil, we are just considering their part in the economy.

The **Crumble Factor** is the ratio of Wasters to Producers.

$$\frac{\text{Wasters}}{\text{Producers}}$$

When the **Crumble Factor** rises to some critical number, the economic structure is in danger of—yes—crumbling.

We are speaking here only of the economic aspect of a society. There are many other ways a society, nation, or even a private company can fail.

The **Crumble Factor** is not a constant for all times and ages; it will vary widely with different societal structures, technology, natural resources, etc. Various societies and cultures throughout history have fallen because they crumbled from within, and when their (individual) critical **Crumble Factor** was reached, a small event would trigger a collapse without participants understanding what happened. They would attribute the Crumble to other factors. External events or pressures to a society or government can expose weaknesses and trigger a **Crumble Factor** collapse as well.

The Mayan culture was one of the great successful civilizations in history, but when they reached their **Crumble Factor**, they crumbled. It could have been an elite ruling class that denigrated some vital occupation, such as farming. A few bad crop years, not enough rain, too many wasters and not enough producers, could have been the cause. We don't know the details. Those who caused the Crumble may have been the same ones who recorded events, and it's unlikely they would tell the whole story if it presented them in a bad light.

Many civilizations and social structures have Crumbled. Typically, an elite ruling class (and the bureaucrat officials) will outgrow and outspend the capability of the Producers. If we only had the data and facts in those cases we might analyze and better understand them. A more recent political organization that Crumbled was the Soviet Union. Numerous interests have been quick to take credit for the demise, but it was the **Crumble Factor** at work. Some say their economy failed to support their military objectives, but that is just another way of saying '**Crumble Factor.**' They realized their limitations soon enough to downsize, and that probably saved them from a total crumble. We should learn from that event.

A similar Crumble Factor can be assigned to industrial companies. The company starts small, grows steadily, matures, and then becomes top-heavy with company bureaucrats and officials. Eventually it will lose its profitability and identity, be absorbed, sell out, or just dissolve. It's almost as if companies have a life cycle like human beings, with their own individual Crumble Factor.

All organizations are susceptible to the **Crumble Factor**. There may be other factors and events, but the basic human nature urge to control will inspire the bureaucratic instinct to assert itself, and the inevitable pattern will devolve. The organization will become top heavy with Wasters at the expense of Producers.

The **Crumble Factor** has modifiers—both numerator and denominator can have multipliers. The role of Producers can be enhanced by better methods, abundant resources, better transportation, and so on. Obviously, modern equipment, better seed, fertilizer, herbicides, and pesticides, will enable one farmer to produce more food today than one farmer could in the past. That type of enhancement has a significant multiplier effect.

Another industry that has had spectacular advancement in productivity is mining. As late as one hundred years ago, underground mining was as labor intensive, perhaps more so, than farming. And politically, mining was respected because all those miners, their families, and suppliers, voted. The difference today is that all that efficient modern equipment does not vote and not as many miners are needed.

Efficiency is eventually taken for granted and then punished by society.

The recent use of computers enhances productivity in ways too numerous to list. On the other hand, computer games may enhance Waster activity.

Modern technology has provided our 'Western Civilization' with unprecedented productivity. This in turn allows our society to support an unprecedented number of Wasters. However, there is some point at which the **Crumble Factor** will become critical. In any society there is a limit to how many Wasters can be supported by the Producers. There will always be a large number of potential Wasters, who will emerge if the possibility exists. Wasters can always waste more, and wasting is an attractive lifestyle for many people.

Wasters can have multiplying factors also, such as, to the extent their standard of living exceeds their basic needs. Many Wasters have higher living standards than their Producers. Some Wasters get fabulously wealthy, but they are still Wasters. They may hire other Wasters to help them, multiplying their Waster effect. If they do not have any intervals of 'production' then all their activities are as Wasters.

The Wasters factor is also increased by interfering with the work of Producers. If some Waster interferes with the production of a Producer, the Waster is having a double effect as a Waster. They not only waste, they inhibit the work of Producers. This leads us to the role government too often plays in the equation when it creates obstacles for producers in the form of laws and regulations.

Bureaucrats

By definition, bureaucrats and entire governments are Wasters. They produce no necessities or useful services. (Government should provide a favorable operating framework for producers.) Bureaucrats and other government officials depend entirely upon the products of producers, and so they are total Wasters.

Every type of social endeavor can use some level of organization, and bureaucrats do provide organization, needed or not. The trouble is, the very drive that makes a good organizer, also carries them past reasonable organization. They don't know when to stop. They firmly believe they can 'order' producers to be more effective and efficient. And they may have some other objective, such as environmentalism. The recent government intrusion into the auto industry is a prime example. The government is forcing the auto companies to 'go green' when there is little or no market for the product. The cost of operating a 'green' car will probably be much more than buying an ordinary car and a lifetime gas supply.

The bureaucrat drive for more and more organization is never satisfied. And more organization means more power and more money for the bureaucracy, money that can only come from Producers.

The 'Green Movement' has produced some unique versions of Wasting. The proposed 'green' activity may waste resources more than the traditional way did. An example is using ethanol in gasoline. Creating the ethanol takes more energy than the energy ethanol produces when used as an additive to gasoline. Check out the farmers who raise the corn used to make the ethanol and see what they put in their tractors.

Another 'penny wise and pound foolish' Waste, is the use of solar cells to generate electricity. The processes used to produce solar cells have a far more deleterious effect on 'the planet' than the benefit they produce. The manufacture of solar cells involves harsh chemicals and toxic processes that are prohibited in this country, so they are manufactured outside this country. Even so, the costly solar cells, as presently manufactured, will never pay for themselves in the electricity they produce. They are only practical in remote areas where conventional supplies of electricity are not available.

The general rule is, "The cheapest way is also the greenest way."

Bureaucrats Rule

Here in the United States we like to think of our nation as the 'cradle of democracy' and that we have a representative system of government. But think about it. If you have a dispute with the government, whom are you disputing with (or to)? The person you voted for won't be much help, and in fact will often decline to get involved. They will say, "You must exhaust the administrative procedures." However, your elected official may have someone look into the matter—some bureaucrat will investigate and report back. The truth of the matter is that our elected officials have little or no control over bureaucrats. Neither elected officials nor bureaucrats want to admit it, but **Bureaucrats Rule**. Even when they are abusive to the public, bureaucrats are protected by civil service laws, and elected officials have no effective power over them. In many cases, elected officials actually fear certain bureaucrat agencies (such as the IRS.) For all practical purposes, we are governed by a bureaucratic dictatorship. In practice, our elected 'representatives' only exist to feed money to the bureaucrats

Whatever the type of government, whether religious, monarchy, dictator, oligarchy, or other, there will be unelected bureaucrats willing to do the bidding of their leader. Of course they will be loyal to their employer; that's where the money is. There will always be bureaucratic types ready to do the bidding of any tyrant, however unethical or immoral it may be.

It is human nature to personify government. The original colonists thought they were rebelling against King George III, but King George never set foot in the colonies. It was his bureaucrats that were the cause of their anger and distress. Based on the information his bureaucrats gave him, the king did make decisions, but his knowledge was limited and slanted by the bias of those very bureaucrats whom he had chosen. We don't know the extent of any misinformation, but history simplifies the situation by personifying the misdeeds to King George III.

Governments, and especially socialist governments, have a symbiotic relationship with bureaucrats. Bureaucrats depend upon the government for employment, and a government that wants to exercise extensive control, an 'ordered' society, needs lots of bureaucrats to enforce that control. And a government that wants to spend lots of money, needs lots of bureaucrats to spend it. 'Central planning' purports to have the solutions for all problems of society, especially economic problems. Central planning requires layers or levels of bureaucrats to pass the decrees from the central government down the chain of command to the working (Producer) people. The Wastefulness of a government is directly proportional to its size.

Jefferson said it most eloquently, "That government is best which governs least."

Retro (grade)

When bureaucrats have enough power to do it, they will
start setting their own goals. Those goals will often be in a
different direction than the original intent of the laws they
are supposedly enforcing. It can even be in the opposite
direction, or **retrograde**. It is often called **Retro**, and
it magnifies their Waster activity. Today's lawmakers
(Congress) have allowed the bureaucrats to make their
own 'laws' which they call 'regulations' and of course the
'regulations' will be in a new direction. If the regulation isn't
in a new direction, why would bureaucrats need a new one?

Over time, a group with a foreign agenda (other than the
will of Congress or the people) can work its way in, and take
control of a government agency. A prime example of this is
the U.S. Forest Service. Their basic charge, upon founding,
was to 'maintain the trails.' Today, their main effort is
to close trails and restrict access. In spite of historic use,
existing laws, and the expressed will of congress, 'greenie'
environmentalists have infiltrated the Forest Service, taken

control, and substituted their own (unadmitted) goals. Their present policy is obviously to prevent any private use of public land. The public will be denied access to public land. This is **retro** to the 'Multiple Use Act' and other expressions of intent enacted by Congress.

There is presently a push by 'greenies' in Congress, with the help of bureaucrats, to designate millions of acres of public land in the Western United States as Wilderness or Wilderness Study areas, so they will be off-limits to any normal public access. Of course this will require more bureaucrats to patrol that Wilderness and give citations to any violators. But they don't tell you it will require more bureaucrats, which of course will cost more money.

They can do this because the United States Congress has abdicated its legislative responsibility and given it to bureaucrats such as the Forest Service. The Forest Service now writes whatever regulations it wants, publishes them in the Federal Register, and then enforces them, as if those regulations were law. To complete the actions of the Forest Service, their fellow 'bureaucrats in black robes' (federal judges) have creatively invented 'Presumption of Regularity.' The 'bureaucrats in black robes' definition of 'presumption of regularity' is that those bureaucrats who wrote the regulations are best qualified to judge how they should be enforced, and in federal court a brother 'bureaucrat in a black robe' will follow the direction of the agency bureaucrats, in this case the Forest Service. So now we have the Forest Service supplanting the three branches of government; legislative, executive, and judicial. The bureaucrat's dream is real for them. They **are** the government. Total control. We have a bureaucratic dictatorship.

The Forest Service takes great pride in fighting Forest fires, and is very effective in playing a sympathetic (echo chamber) news media with extensive coverage in which the Forest Service is always of course, the heroic good guys.

Reporters for the news media usually have a 'Slant' when they report a story. It may be personal bias or knowledge of what their bosses want, or a combination of the two. (They probably were hired by people who knew what their 'Slant' would be.) It can also be called 'Conclusionary Reporting' which would be the case if they already had a predetermined conclusion which would fit the preferred 'Slant.' At its best, Conclusionary Reporting is an attempt to color an event to make it interesting. At its worst, Conclusionary Reporting is a deliberate attempt to report (or even invent) facts to promote an agenda or withhold facts critical to the true story. A classic case of Conclusionary Reporting was that of Margaret Mead, who wrote books on anthropology about the South Seas 'primitive' societies. It turned out that the subjects she was writing about, figured out what she wanted to hear and 'slanted' their comments and stories to please her. Her conclusions have since been widely discredited.

However, there is another side to their story the Forest Service doesn't want the public to know.

The largest fire in the history of Colorado, was set by Forest Service personnel.

The largest fire in the history of New Mexico was set by Forest Service personnel.

The largest fire in the history of Arizona was set by an unemployed firefighter who wanted a job with the Forest Service fighting fires.

One busy year, for fighting fires so gallantly, Congress gave an extra $700 million to the Forest Service.

The bureaucratic mind sees clearly that the more and bigger fires it has, the more money it gets.

Another example of bureaucratic dictatorship, is the Interior Board of Land Appeals, or the I.B.L.A. This author tried to find out more information about who is on the board, what their qualifications are, when the board meets, where it meets, how qualified the members are, and who appoints the members of the board. I could find out **NOTHING**. Apparently this is a secret board, with secret members, who meet at a secret time in a secret place, to make their final decisions. This is the ultimate bureaucratic 'administration' of land control. Nothing about the board or its members is available to the public. This is typical of bureaucrats; they do not want the public to know what they are doing behind the scene. What are they trying to hide? And why?

We suspect that the bureaucrat administrators of the recent 'Obama healthcare bill' will look to the Interior Board of Land Appeals procedure for inspiration as a model to emulate in place of death panels. A panel would imply a mock hearing, and some degree of publicity, and might be noticed by the general public. The last thing bureaucrats want is public exposure. The 'Obama healthcare bill' was written by—who? We challenge anyone to reveal the names of the bureaucrats who wrote it and disclose what part of the bill they are responsible for.

There are other federal bureaucrats in other federal agencies that are wasting the Producers money, and on a more local level there are state bureaucrats that are wasting the state's money, but you get the picture. Bureaucrats are full time Wasters, and the more of them there are and the more power they have, the more they can Waste. And of course they will continue to strive for anonymity.

The Hidden Party

Some bureaucrats are sympathetic to the Democrat Party, some are sympathetic to the Republican party, but all are loyal to the unseen **Bureaucrat Party**.

Ironically, the **Bureaucrat Party** is not organized as a party. The **Bureaucrat Party** is more of a 'Colloquial Attitude' than an identifiable organization, and it works by personal contact in addition to circulating resumes. Those employed and entrenched bureaucrats hire their like-minded friends. (Colloquial Attitudes are mutually agreed upon opinions shared by a group of people with common interests. The group is typically in a common geographic area, but can be a group of like-minded people over a large area.)

In this United States, the main headquarters of the **Bureaucrat Party** is in the Washington D.C. area, but there is not a definable building or group of people making up the headquarters. There are similar headquarters in the vicinity of each state capital, and then there are supporting bureaucrats all across the country and nations all around the world. They view themselves as the 'Ruling Class'. They share the common belief that their (important) job is to govern and control the less capable for their own good, and in the interest of efficiency and smooth operations.

The Bureaucrat Party is effectively, at this time, as permanent as any government can be. Elected politicians may come and go, but the bureaucrats are there for their lifetime. They may rotate into and out of positions, depending on the party in power, but they can always find a government job. We may elect representatives who have good intentions, but when they report to serve, they are surrounded by professional lifetime bureaucrats, who will steer them in the 'approved' direction. The information our representatives receive will be filtered by the bureaucrats.

There are various means of holding the bureaucrats together, but the most pervasive is money. An attitude that they are more knowledgeable and smarter than the general public, is pervasive at all levels of bureaucracy. And they expect to be amply rewarded for their expertise.

Federal bureaucrats have the greatest access to money and therefore the greatest influence on other bureaucrats and agencies, and even private individuals and organizations, both in our own country and abroad.

The most obvious money influence is direct grants, set up by federal bureaucrats for other bureaucrats and friendly 'private' groups and individuals. NGO's or Non-Governmental-Organizations are a common favorite for grants. These are seldom productive and must be classed as total Wasters. Too often it is just a way of government bureaucrats rewarding their supporters. The story of abuse in this area is beyond the scope of this book, or probably any single book.

A less obvious, but perennial class of 'quiet' grants is **PILT**, Payment In Lieu of Taxes. The federal government owns major portions of many states in the West, and does not pay property taxes, but does make payments (grants) to local governments. Counties and states have little or no leverage with the federal bureaucrats making **PILT** payments, but the locals gladly accept the money, even with strings attached. This in turn makes them dependent on the largess of the federal bureaucrats. Local governments are not going to bite the federal hand that feeds them. In this way, federal bureaucrats, using their generosity with **OPM** (Other Peoples Money), gain the control needed to push their agendas on the state and local levels. The recipients are of course beholden to their friendly federal bureaucrats instead of the Producers who are really providing the money.

Another area where influence of federal bureaucrats is strong, is with law enforcement. Federal agents can offer free materials and training for state and local police and sheriffs' deputies. However, one of the things taught in police academies is that all federal officials are 'brother officers' which has very strong implications. This means that local law enforcement, when called to any event, will accept a federal employee's statements as fact. Remember this if you have any dispute, or worse yet an altercation, with a federal employee. The local law enforcement has been trained to accept what a federal employee says as true fact, over anything you say and in spite of what conditions may actually exist. Your local sheriff, supposedly the highest ranking lawman in the county, is likely beholden to federal bureaucrats, and will do what the federal bureaucrats tell him.

Federal bureaucrats have created a network of dependency all over our country and much of the world, using **OPM** (Other Peoples Money.) This has an enormous effect on the **Crumble Factor**. When money or goods are sent out of the country and no benefit is received here, it's as if the money or goods were dumped into a big black hole. That good production just disappeared and is gone as far as local use is concerned. Waster government bureaucrats have just destroyed some Producer's work. Some Wasters may say it eases our collective guilty conscience, but that is of no consequence to the **Crumble Factor**. The **Crumble Factor** is neutral; it is not concerned with good or bad intentions.

Planning is the 'forte' of Bureaucrats

(In musical terminology, 'forte' means 'loud.')

Politicians and bureaucrats delight in planning. They see it as their big opportunity to determine the future (using OPM) the way they want the future to be. But nobody can really plan for the future. Recent natural disasters show that dramatically. We seldom know what the future will be, so bureaucrats actually plan for the past, because their plans have to be based on past events.

Economists also have plans. Their training is based on theories, which in turn, are based on past events. To prove their theories, they have to get their hot little hands on the levers of power, to test their theories and control events the way they think events should happen. They easily merge and share their beliefs and theories with politicians and bureaucrats, who are also trying to control future conditions and events. The common belief which they share, is that the government can and should control events. Particularly, economic events and economic activity. They would do this with nationwide and even worldwide control by Central Planning. They will not repeat the mistakes of the past. (They will make their own *new* mistakes.)

'Central Planning' is the opposite of the democratic process. Government controlled Central Planning is a top-down type of organization. A democratic process would allow input from the bottom to go up to the government leaders. Central Planners and other autocrats sometimes stage 'demonstrations' to give the illusion of popular support, but mob-rule is not democracy. The bureaucrats often ask for 'public input' when in actuality they have predetermined the decision themselves, and the public's input is ignored. Planners may use the status quo, but today's status quo is tomorrow's past.

Planners cannot predict technical breakthroughs, although they can prevent them with short-sighted policies.

Nobody could predict Tesla would invent the AC electric system used all over the world today. Even the great inventor Edison did not believe it was better than DC electric systems. Yet, the conditions were such that under the free enterprise/capitalist system it could be developed and promoted. Today it is the foundation of our civilization. Under a bureaucratically controlled system, a project of such enormity would never have been allowed.

Nobody could predict that two bicycle mechanics from Ohio would be the first to fly, but under the free enterprise conditions prevailing at the time, the Wright brothers did.

Nobody could predict that an obscure patent clerk in Germany would become the world's leading theoretician, but Einstein did it.

Neither bureaucrat planners, nor anyone else, can predict what will happen in a free society, and that is more than an Achilles heel to bureaucratic central planning. They cannot plan for the future if the future is unknown, but that doesn't keep them from pretending to know the future and how to plan for it.

The Secret of Success

This leads us to the **Secret of Success** for the 'American Experiment.' Democracy was the most obvious definitive characteristic of the 'American Experiment' but there was another equally important innovation that quickly became the basis for economic progress, and that was, and still is, the **Patent System** operating in a **free enterprise system**. Previously, the sovereign would grant a patent to a friend or political favorite for a monopoly of some sort, usually of a lucrative financial nature. The **Patent System** and **individual freedom**, in combination, have led to the world's most productive society, which is today the envy of the world. But the world doesn't see the whole picture, it sees only the democracy part. And there is not much chance that authoritarian regimes will imitate the 'free enterprise' part, even if they want to imitate the American success, because they fear individual personal freedom.

The idea that individual citizens, with no political favoritism, could obtain even a temporary monopoly for a useful innovation, was as dramatic a change as democracy itself. A spirit of invention for personal profit developed, which exists to this day. (A beneficial Colloquial Attitude.) It takes only one example of commercial success to inspire others, just as it took only one rich gold strike to start a gold rush. (And a gold rush could happen again today.)

Patents, Trademarks, and Copyrights, along with the free enterprise system, are the foundation on which America's great success is based. When constructive and more efficient innovation is rewarded, it will thrive and inspire and encourage others. If innovation is ignored, or even punished, there will be more downshifters and the status quo will become stagnant.

Innovation has not always been rewarded. The first 'steam engine' was really a water pump used to drain mines in England. There was no piston, only a tank submersed in the water, one way inlet and outlet valves at the bottom, and a control valve for the steam at the top of the tank. To operate, someone had to open the steam control valve to let the steam into the tank, so that the steam pressure pushed water down in the tank, through the (one way) outlet valve into the drain pipe, and out of the mine. Then the steam valve was closed, the steam in the tank quickly condensed to water, taking up less space, the pressure dropped, and water came into the tank through the (one way) inlet valve at the bottom, rising in the tank. The process was then repeated, and repeated, and repeated. It was boring work, but not strenuous. All that was required was to turn the steam valve open and closed at the proper time. Ideal for child labor. A boy was hired to do the job. An innovative boy, he devised a mechanism that would automatically turn the steam valve on and off at the proper time in the sequence. This allowed the boy to simply watch the 'steam engine' work. Since he could just sit and watch the 'engine' work automatically, he got bored and fell asleep. They caught him sleeping on the job, so they boxed his ears and sent him home. (Fired him.) He had invented a control system for the pump, but he was sleeping on the job. In better times, he would have been rewarded for his innovative improvement. As it was, he must have become a downshifter, because today his identity is unknown.

Most other countries in the world today don't get the significance of rewarding utilitarian innovation; they think success comes with 'democracy' and so they imitate the appearance of democracy. Some of the staged 'democratic elections' by tyrannical governments are tragically amusing. They apparently feel the need to be 'validated' by their constituents, at least in the eyes of the outside world. But democracy is not the 'endgoal' it is only the means (hopefully) to the endgoal of individual freedom.

The **Secret of Success** for the American Experiment is not just democratic elections where everybody votes, it is more importantly the reward for utilitarian innovation, as expressed in our Patent and Copyright systems. Innovators can be rewarded with a time limited monopoly for a worthwhile contribution to society. When that happens, it encourages others who may not immediately contribute something, but they feel the warm possibility that it *could* happen to them. And they may be able to improve on the innovation, to their own benefit. They feel a personal association and trust in the system. They are optimistic about technological progress and their own future.

Individual freedom, in all aspects, requires a society free of government (bureaucratic) restriction. This is in sharp contrast to the bureaucratic ideal of the 'ordered' society. The most successful government will be the one that can balance the two, providing a minimal structure that permits maximum personal innovation. A general **Colloquial Attitude** of freedom of expression and appreciation of any contribution made, engenders an optimism favoring innovation. The innovators of the American Experiment, our 'Founding Fathers,' succeeded beyond their expectations by their understanding of human nature. We would be wise to study the ideologies they had and restore them today, if we wish continued success for the American Experiment.

High Play

"High Play" is the title of a book by Harmon Bro that is a study in group dynamics. He describes 'high play' as being a group effort of like minded individuals working together on a project toward a common goal. They set aside their personal priorities for their collective goal. It sounds familiar, doesn't it? Something like personal submission to the collective, for the greater good.

High Play and communal success are critically dependent on the individual's enthusiasm. As long as there is personal, individual interest in the group, it can work. However, once the individuals lose eye contact, personal interest comes back in, to the detriment of the group effort. Bureaucrat types will always step forward to control any organization. Eventually, they will assume power and ride on the back of the organization, for their own benefit and exaltation. Mere individual members will soon see conflict with the leaders, even though the leaders will try to glorify themselves and identify with the original purpose. High play can work in small groups, but will likely fail when bureaucrats, at some remote distance, take over and run things for their own goals.

Downshifters

"**Downshifter**" is a name given to individuals who could achieve and produce more, but chose not to. They live a simpler, less productive life for various reasons. This has a significant effect on the **Crumble Factor**. Many 'downshifters' resent taxes taking a large part of their salary (their production.) They intentionally limit their income to stay in a lower tax bracket. It would be difficult to say what production they would have, because they don't even try to excel. They may decline to form a company and expand their production because of all the bureaucratic 'red tape.'

Downshifters see many of the bureaucrats and other Wasters living well without producing, resent it, and do not want to support it. They intentionally limit their production, reducing the denominator in the **Crumble Factor**, driving the **Crumble Factor** higher.

Downshifters are the downfall of socialism. They can't be forced to produce according to their ability, because no one knows what their maximum ability is, or even who the Downshifters are. Just like you can't push on a string, especially when you don't even know where the string is.

The best thing government can do is provide a favorable environment for all people and hope the Downshifters will emerge and contribute. Socialistic Bureaucrats don't understand the concept of Downshifters and don't have a clue as to the mindset of Downshifters; it is unnatural to them. The Bureaucrats core belief is control, and the unbridled thought processes of innovators is beyond their comprehension.

The real **Secret of Success** behind the American Experiment was (and is) providing the framework that allows the innovators to perform, and encouraging them with the attraction of personal reward. Authoritarian systems will never allow the required freedom.

Further proof is the success many foreigners have when they come to this United States, believing it to be the 'Land of Opportunity,' and they achieve success for themselves.

Downshifters exist at all levels, from high Producers to low Producers. Many Wasters, who could be Producers, will take the line of least resistance if they can be provided with 'welfare.' Their multiplier in the **Crumble Factor** moves from Producer to Waster. Why work if they can draw money without working? Also, too many Wasters can 'swamp out' the Producers at the polls on election day, and elect politicians who reward Wasters. 'Entitlements' have become a political and monetary reward that will determine how many of the Wasters vote. Many Wasters firmly believe they are entitled to the production of the Producers. Bureaucrats and many politicians encourage that belief for *their* benefit and reelection.

Charity is one thing, but the other side of charity is appreciation of the gift. If the 'gift' is demanded, it is not charity, it is confiscation. There is more charity in the tip you spontaneously leave a waitress than in taking a tax deduction for 'charity' to get a tax break. The tax deduction is a business deal with the tax collector. When the government takes your production and gives it to someone else, there is no charity involved.

There is little doubt that the United States government, in 2011, is raising the **Crumble Factor** to dangerous levels. We have described the **Crumble Factor** in general terms without getting into a lot of specifics, but there is a plethora of instances contributing to an excess of Wasters.

But the question remains, how can we reduce the **Crumble Factor**? If we want to reduce the chance of crumbling, we must reduce the number of Wasters and/or reduce their effectiveness, and increase the number of Producers and/or their effectiveness. If we could change Wasters to Producers and change **Downshifters** to better Producers, it would have a large effect in reducing the **Crumble Factor**.

Our government, without shame, manipulates individual incentives with taxes, and causes unexpected effects such as **Downshifters**. But what if tax laws could be used on older people to encourage them to continue to produce? What if, instead of applying for Social Security, they could continue producing but at a lower tax rate? Would a 10% lower tax rate do it? 20%? How about zero income taxes if they work after 80 years of age? Or 75 years of age? We could have an income tax that is **progressively lower** with age. That would be truly progressive.

It might also be beneficial to have a lower tax rate for the young producers. Why not have a low tax bracket for those under twenty years of age? Or under twenty five years? Not much would be lost in tax revenue because those are not high income years for most individuals. However, they would be encouraged to become high Producers.

!!! Repeal WHAT?? !!

Back in the thirties (you know—the Great Depression) and before that, we had the 'Spoils System' for government workers instead of Civil Service. The winners of the election would take the 'spoils of victory', that is the government jobs.

The chief executive typically hired members of his (her) own party to be the bureaucrats. Roosevelt, a democrat, hired fellow democrats to run the post offices and other government agencies. If you got a republican president, you could expect to see republican postmasters and government workers.

On the state level, the governor similarly hired state employees (bureaucrats) from his (her) own party. In many states, it's still that way.

That's the way it was, and it worked fairly well.

The bureaucrats knew that, indirectly, their job depended on pleasing the voters. If the public perception was that they were doing a poor job, or being abusive to the public, chances were that the next election would put them out of a job. Then the other party would take over and supply new and hopefully better workers. The government workers had a practical, personal interest in serving the public well. Their own job depended on it.

A state or city highway department's work is quite visible to the public. One of the most obvious duties of that department is removing snow in the winter. The bureaucrat's success in that endeavor is taken by the public as the effectiveness of the government, and more than one party has been thrown out of office for failure to keep the streets cleaned off in the winter.

Enter Civil Service. Bureaucrats would be secure in their government jobs, regardless of which party was in power. The government would hire only the best, because, and because—, and—. And they would bla—and bla—.

It isn't working like it was supposed to. Government bureaucrats have become more arrogant, dictatorial, and abusive to the public, in addition to being overpaid. (Independent surveys have shown that federal workers are paid significantly higher salaries than workers doing similar tasks in the private sector.) In Colorado a federal food service worker can get a higher salary than the governor of the state.

If we repealed Civil Service, there is a good chance that the size of the federal government would be much reduced. There is also a good chance that government spending would be much reduced—all those bureaucrats cost and spend MONEY. The fewer bureaucrats, the less money spent.

Most people will agree that efficiency is desperately needed in government. One novel way to inspire bureaucrats would be to have them take Forced Sabbaticals. They would be required to take an unpaid leave, perhaps a year, without pay. If they were worth the pay they had been getting as a government employee, they would have no trouble getting an equivalent or even better job in private industry. If they were truly as exceptional as their government pay indicated, they would be a boon to the private sector and contribute mightily to an economic boom. They might even become Producers instead of Wasters.

Perhaps it would take amendments to the U.S. Constitution, but we should ban grants or transfers of money between government bodies, except for services rendered. State and local governments should stand on their own resources. If their own taxpayers won't support a project, the project probably shouldn't be done. Too many politicians look at federal money as free money—it isn't. It comes from somebody's production.

States should be allowed to compete with each other in as many areas as possible. If one state wants to tax Producers heavily and give the money to another group (read Wasters and party supporters) it could do that. Another state might be friendly to Producers and less generous to Wasters. It wouldn't take long for things to even out. The states favoring good Producers would soon have good Producers and the states favoring Wasters would soon have lots of Wasters. **Downshifters** would prefer states that appreciated their Production.

There are many activities that can be performed more efficiently by states than the federal government, and there are many activities that can be performed more efficiently by cities and counties than by the states in which they are located. In general, the more local the government performing the activity, the more efficient it is likely to be. If local tax money is spent locally, there is a chance local voters can monitor the process. It is foolish to tax at the local level, send the money to Washington, and then let the federal bureaucrats send it back to the locality to be spent on activities that may be antithetical to those taxed. Similarly, on a state level, it is foolish to send money to the state capital and then have state bureaucrats send money back to the local level where the taxes came from. This would be in direct conflict with the bureaucrat dream, because it removes the power they would have of rewarding their friends and funding their own goals.

In the perfect bureaucratic dream of the 'ordered society' there would be an all inclusive code which must be obeyed, and which would control every possible situation. Each would produce according to ability, but bureaucrats don't know about **Downshifters**, and wouldn't know what to do about them if they did know. **Downshifters** upset the whole idea of any 'high play' because they will limit their participation. They don't like to be taken for granted and carry drones. And how would bureaucrats know who was downshifting?

There is a story of a man who worked in a railroad yard, and always carried a large pipe wrench on his shoulder. From the size of the pipe wrench, you would expect that he was going some place to work or returning from using that big wrench. Actually, the most work he ever did was to carry the pipe wrench around all day. But he looked like he was going to work any minute. How would a bureaucrat know the difference?

In contrast, there are indications that some elements of 'high play' are taking place today in the 'Tea Party' (which in fact, is not a party, but a movement.)

Both the Republican Party and the Democrat Party are top-down organizations, which is the accepted bureaucratic concept. The few elite leaders at the top make the decisions and pass them down to the lower, lesser members. Those lower in the ranks are not to question, they are to follow and not criticize or even offer suggestions.

The Tea Party, if you can even call it a Party, is an inverse to the Republican and Democrat parties. It is not top-down, it is more a bottoms-up movement. The individual is totally independent, and many members disagree significantly with each other, but they do have some common opinions (Colloquial Attitudes) even though they may disagree on the best way to achieve their common interests.

The Tea Parties are an interesting variation of Harmon Bro's 'High Play' because the common goals are nationwide and the individual members are spread across the country, and even the world. They don't personally know many of the other like-minded individuals, but they share common beliefs and goals.

STEALTH TAXES

There are many 'Stealth' Taxes' hidden in the prices we pay for things. Most are on a fixed basis and often plainly marked, such as your telephone bill, the gasoline price, etc. But the most hidden of the stealth taxes is inflation.

Ask the old-timers. They can tell you they remember when a quarter of a dollar, a 25 cent coin, would buy a gallon of gas and a candy bar. Gas was 19.9 cents per gallon and a candy bar was five cents, a nickel.

What can you buy with that quarter today?

Actually, you can buy more. That was a **silver** quarter. If you check the price of silver quarters, you will see that you would have more than enough to buy a gallon of gas and a candy bar.

In 1937 you could buy a brand new Plymouth automobile, basic transportation with a heater (no radio) for $750. With gold at $35 per ounce, that was about 21 ounces of gold. Today, 21 ounces of gold at $1500 per ounce would be worth

$31,500. If you had 21 ounces of gold today, you could buy even more than basic transportation.

Someone once said you could buy a good man's suit with 1 ounce of gold. Back in the days when gold was $35 per ounce, you could buy a good man's suit for that amount. Today with the price of gold above $1,500 per ounce, you can buy a *great* man's suit with 1 ounce of gold.

The difference between today's price and the 'old' price is what inflation took away from us. Government takes more away from us by inflation than it does with taxes. And when the federal government inflates, people blame each other, not the real culprit, our own federal government.

Opponents to gold and silver backing argue that there is not enough gold and silver to back the currency presently in circulation. Of course not, if you are talking about the old ($35 per ounce) ratio, but as you can see from the examples above, there is a new ratio for backing paper money. At this writing, gold is selling for about $1500 per ounce. That is, 1500 paper federal notes are needed to buy an ounce of gold. The **moneychangers** have taken $1465 away from the price of an ounce of gold. ($1500—$35) Talk about inflation!! The **moneychangers** have secretly taxed us by inflation to the extent of 42.86 (1500 divided by 35) or 4286% !! It's even worse if you use the base of $20.67 per ounce that was the world price before Roosevelt called in all the gold in the United States. That would be (1500 divided by 20 = 75) giving roughly 7500% inflation !!

An interesting example: If you had purchased a one ounce gold coin when you could get one for $35 and held it all this time, you could sell it today for $1500+. You would have a 'capital gain' of $1465, *and have to pay taxes on it !!* Most people would agree, yes, you had a capital gain and you should pay the tax. This shows a change in the commonly accepted **monetary frame of reference** now based on **Fake money**. This is a serious distortion of reality. The gold has not changed; it is still the same as it was, but the perception is that the price of it has increased.

The **monetary frame of reference** can be compared to riding a speeding, accelerating train. We know that the train is moving relative to the earth. After a while, when we look out the window, we think of the scenery as 'going by' and that *we* are stable. Our frame of reference has changed.

The true **monetary frame of reference**, based on real money, is gold. Otherwise, we have an ever changing, unstable base. To have a **monetary frame of reference** based on a moving paper dollar, is a deception that will lead to widespread economic distortions. And what is more scary is that the monetary train, driven by the **moneychangers** in the locomotive, is *accelerating* !! How much more can it accelerate, and where will it stop? Will we be in another country?

The **moneychanger**/politicians in Washington have gradually and surreptitiously substituted their **Fake**, fiat money for our Constitutional gold and silver money. The resulting inflation and economic distress are a result of their deception and perfidy. For our own well-being and the good of our nation, we must force a return to Constitutional money. And maybe we should start calling the senators and congressmen in Washington '**moneychangers**' instead of senator or congressman, for the bait-and—switch operation they have pulled off.

Inflation is presently the largest tax ever put on the American people, and much more than King George ever dreamed of, but nobody blames the **moneychangers**. And the culprits (**moneychangers**) aren't going to tell you or admit what they did. The closest they will come to admitting it, is to blame their predecessor **moneychangers**.

Gold and silver are reality. There is a limited, finite supply available for use at any given time. If paper money ('receipts') is limited by the supply of gold and silver, the government is limited in the amount of inflation it can cause. This is very distasteful to the **moneychangers**, who would rather raise money using inflation than raise taxes on the people. The **moneychangers** have gradually reduced the amount of gold and silver backing for our paper money so they can use inflation to get their spending money instead of using an honest but unpleasant method, that is, raising taxes.

By removing *all* gold and silver backing, the **money-changers** have no limitations on the amount of money they can create with inflation. They have an unlimited amount of money they can print. The 'Gutenberg Solution' has solved their spending problem.

Once, in a restaurant, years ago, there was a commotion among the waitresses. After it was over and things settled down, one of the customers asked, "What was that fuss all about?" The answer was "Oh, somebody left a real dime."

Waitresses are not students of monetary legerdemain, but they know a real dime when they see one.

Before the U.S. Government removed gold and silver from coinage, it issued gold and silver certificates; paper 'demand' notes that stated that the government would pay 'on demand' the equivalent amount of gold or silver, corresponding to the face value of the certificate. There was no time limit or other requirement. The American dollar was 'as good as gold.' This, and the known gold reserves at Fort Knox, gave the world confidence that they could hold American paper dollars instead of having to hold, and protect from thieves, physical gold. The American dollar became the 'reserve' currency for the world. Nations could hold American paper dollars much easier than physical gold bars.

During the Lyndon Johnson presidency, there was a 'run' on the gold certificates. Other nations turned in millions of paper dollar certificates to get physical gold from the United States at $35 per ounce. Some foreign countries then melted down the gold to make their own gold coins which they sold worldwide for $100 per ounce (the gold price on the free market.) And at the time, Americans were not allowed to own gold at all, and American gold miners were forced to sell gold to the United States Mint at $35 per ounce. The **moneychangers** had effectively taken $65 (100-35) from each $100 owned by Americans. Johnson's bureaucrat advisers told him that dumping all the United States' gold on the world market would force the price down, and the government could buy it back at a lower price. Instead of forcing the price of gold lower as Johnson's advisers predicted, the federal bureaucrats had to stop redeeming the certificates or face the possibility of an empty Fort Knox. The United States Government opted to lie and not redeem the certificates that promised to pay in gold. Our government LIES. It now prints paper dollar 'notes' that do not promise anything but more paper notes. It is **Fake Money**. The **moneychangers** pulled it off without anybody noticing.

REAL MONEY is made of gold and silver. The Constitution says so because the founders who wrote our Constitution knew what real money was (and still is.) **REAL MONEY** has a 'Store of Value' and also a **real** or 'intrinsic' value if it is melted down for the metal in it. The founders had seen what **Fake Money** does to the economy and the nation. They had personal and disappointing experience with paper money. Individual banks had issued paper money and eventually failed, leaving the paper worthless. Even the Central government, had issued paper money which also soon became worthless. The phrase 'Not worth a Continental' was fresh in their memories. (The Continental Congress, which preceded our present Constitution, issued paper money with no gold or silver redeeming feature. It soon became worthless.) The founders learned much more quickly than present day **moneychangers** who are carrying on the charade.

Fake Money causes inflation. Today, the quarter (of a dollar) coin is not made of silver, it's made of nickel and copper and costs pennies to make. It's not worth melting down, because the alloy is not that useful. The government's cost for quarters is pennies, and it sells them to you and me for almost 10 times their cost. The government prints paper money for even greater profits. The government can print notes of one dollar, ten dollars, twenty dollars, fifty dollars, and one hundred dollars, and higher, each of which costs only pennies to make. And what is a note? A note is a debt, to be paid at some future (unspecified) time. How do the **moneychangers** circumvent the Constitution, which clearly specifies gold and silver coinage? Bureaucrats in black robes have cleared the way. If they were honest, the government would replace "In God We Trust" with "Ha Ha Ha" because the **Fake Money** is a cruel joke on a trusting public. But inflation is only one part of the story.

Psychologists tell us that people can only think of one thing at a time, multitasking notwithstanding. Years ago, planners realized this and added the progressive income tax to our system. The progressive income tax, as we all know, specifies higher percentages or 'brackets' of tax liability as income rises.

These tax brackets are fixed to specific ranges of income; as your income increases, you move to a higher bracket and pay a higher percentage of your income (Production.)

With inflation, incomes must be higher to maintain the same standard of living, but the income increase (in **Fake Money**) pushes us into higher brackets of taxation. People think they're getting more money, which they are, but the **Fake Money** they get buys less. However, they moved to a higher tax bracket and are paying a **higher percentage** of their income in taxes. They are paying a higher percentage of their income for the same standard of living. They must 'run harder' and pay higher taxes, just to stay at the same standard of living.

In 1950, a schoolteacher's starting salary was $2000—per year!!! The federal tax on that income for a single person with no dependents was $65, or 3 1/4%. School teachers today are making many times that starting salary, but what percentage are they paying in taxes? Ask any schoolteacher. Such are the wonders of inflation and the progressive income tax. Another **stealth tax** is sneaking up on us.

The combination of inflation and the progressive income tax, creates another **stealth tax.**

People don't notice inflation if it's a small percentage each year. But over a period of many years, and with fixed taxation brackets, people are gradually pushed into higher and higher percentages of taxation. (Even some of the 'banana republics' let people 'index' to inflation, which lessens the 'bracket creep.')

Of course occasionally, in later years the Washington **moneychangers** can generously, and with great fanfare, lower the percentages in each bracket—slightly, but knowing that not too far in the future, continued inflation will increase revenue to the government.

It's a beautiful plan—for the federal **moneychangers** and those who work for the federal government. What makes it even more beautiful for them is that people blame each other (and Producers) for inflation. Very few blame the federal government, even though the federal **moneychangers** are diluting the money supply by injecting '**fake money**.' It's money that was not earned or taken by taxes, it was just created by declaring it to be money. In business it's called 'watering the stock' and would be illegal if you or I tried it.

And it's a way to screw the old people on fixed incomes and punish those nasty individuals who would try to save money. It erodes the value of what they thought they had saved.

If we analyze 'progressive' income tax with Government Doublespeak we can see that realistically it would be a 'regressive' income tax, not progressive. Ironically, it has the greatest percentage tax increase in the lower brackets !! As they get more money, but maintain the same standard of living, they get pushed up into higher brackets faster. It is a disincentive to productive people and depressive to economic development.

The **Stealth Taxes** are an insult and cruel hoax on the people. The ironic and unfair thing is that inflation is blamed on everybody except the federal **moneychangers**. The news media can report that "the XYZ company is raising the price of—whatever" and nobody blames the **moneychangers** in Congress. They blame the XYZ company. They blame the symptom instead of the cause. If doctors treated the symptom instead of the cause, we would all be in poor health, but the federal **moneychangers**, add to the deception by blaming the high price of commodities on the greedy XYZ companies.

The federal **moneychangers** in Congress cause inflation by creating **FAKE MONEY**, and then somebody else gets blamed. Beautiful.

We are on a runaway inflation train, and the **money-changers** in Washington are still giving it full throttle.

Banks are controlled by the Federal Government, and they do their part with a system called 'Fractional Reserve' banking.

Fractional (Reserve) Banking

Gold and silver coins are a convenient, concentrated store of value. This also makes them a prime target for thieves. In medieval times, this was a problem for merchants and traders. The goldsmiths supplied an answer. They would store the coins, and issue a receipt, for a small fee. The next step, was to let the receipt be traded, as if it were the gold coin itself. A merchant could purchase goods with the receipt for gold, and the seller could redeem the receipt for gold from the goldsmith. It became a popular method for trade and contributed to the growth of mercantilism. The receipt was even easier to carry and protect, than the gold coin.

The practice became widespread. The goldsmiths soon had lots of gold coins, and the receipts were traded as if they were gold coins. Then the goldsmiths noticed that not many people were redeeming the receipts for the gold coins. And some enterprising goldsmiths decided they could issue more gold receipts as loans, without gold coin backing, and charge interest on them, because it was unlikely that everyone would want their gold coins at once. The goldsmiths were so appreciative, they stopped charging a fee. The gold coins were 'fungible' which is another way of saying they were indistinguishable from each other. You probably wouldn't get back the same coin you lent the goldsmith, but it wouldn't matter because the coin you received had the same value as the one you had left with the goldsmith. Soon, the value of the gold receipts in circulation exceeded the value of the gold coins held by the goldsmiths. This was the start of what is today called fractional-reserve banking.

Today, banks have taken the place of the goldsmiths. Today, what they call 'reserves' has taken the place of the gold coins. The lending of 'receipts,' however, is now the most important revenue producing activity and what was 'receipts' is now the current 'money.' The name 'fractional-reserve' comes from the practice of lending out more in loans than the fraction that is held in 'reserve' (deposits) in the bank. This works fine for the bank, as long as the owners of the reserves do not all demand return of their money at the same time. If the owners of the 'reserves' all demand their money at the same time, it is called a 'run' on the bank, and the bank will not have enough money to satisfy all of its depositors. Needless to say, a 'run' is not a happy time for the banks or the depositors, because the bank must find money to replace what they owe, or declare they are in default.

Banks have what many would call an upside-down version of definitions. They call loans 'assets,' and the deposits are 'liabilities.' This makes sense if you consider that assets produce revenue for the banks, and liabilities are obligations to repay money to depositors (lenders) sometime in the future. But bankers don't like the sound of 'liabilities,' so the 'liabilities' are called 'reserves.' When you deposit money in a bank, they add it to their 'reserves.' Your deposit is now a 'reserve' for the bank, but they still owe you that amount of money.

Let's take an example. Suppose you deposit one dollar in your bank. The bank can then lend out ten dollars at say 5% interest. (This is typical interest.) The bank will be getting a total of $.50 interest on the ten dollars loaned out, using your one dollar deposit. (In two years they would get one dollar interest, equaling your deposit.) This is great for the bank, and the borrowers are happy to get a loan. But what happens if one of the borrowers goes broke and can't repay the dollar borrowed from the bank? The bank just lost your dollar.

Meanwhile, your neighbor put one dollar in another bank. The other bank can lend out ten dollars. If your neighbor's bank deposits one dollar into your bank, then your bank's reserve is doubled. Your bank can loan ten dollars more. Your bank appreciates the loan so much, that it deposits one of those dollars in your neighbor's bank. Your neighbor's bank now has two dollars on deposit, and can lend out twenty dollars. Your bank also has two dollars on deposit and can lend out twenty dollars. Your dollar and your neighbor's dollar have generated almost forty dollars, not just twenty dollars. This is one way banks can help each other build up their reserves. (In most cases, the banks will borrow money cheaper from the Federal Reserve, but that is really just another bank, albeit a really big one.) Everybody is rich and happy and the bank looks to be in great shape, but looks can be deceiving. Banks have so many ways of building up reserves, that just knowing the assets and reserves ratio is not always a true indicator of the financial status of the bank.

Fractional-reserve banking is the accepted practice today, but the fraction varies. It is obvious that the 'assets' to 'reserves' ratio can be an indication of two very different things.

The first thing to the bankers, is the possibility of more revenue from interest if the ratio is high. The more money loaned out, the more interest the bank makes, and interest is the banks' major source of revenue. Bankers are tempted to make more and more loans, even if some of the loans are risky. The banks are hopeful that some higher authority will come in to save them if the loans go bad. Or maybe they can sell the bad loans to somebody else. Or they can buy insurance, even if the insurance is inadequate. The banks want to look solid and dependable so others will deposit their money like you did. And they want you to keep your money there too, so they may give you a little (very little) interest. They would be getting fifty cents interest based on your dollar deposit, but they would give you very little interest, a few pennies if you're lucky.

The second thing is a possible danger signal; a high ratio indicates that more loans and higher value loans have been made. There are bound to be some that are more risky than others. If some borrowers default or stop paying interest, the bank can be in trouble. The 'leverage' of fractional-reserve banking works both ways, and depending on the ratio, when it's good, it's very good for the banks, and when it's bad, it can be devastating.

When economic conditions are good, banks are flush with cash and anxious to make loans—that's what they make money on. But when economic conditions turn sour, many of the loans they made in more optimistic times, also turn sour. Borrowers may have trouble paying the interest, and have no possible chance of paying off the loan, ever. When borrowers stop paying interest, their loan is called a 'non-performing asset.' Often the bank will still list the loan as an asset, even when it knows the loan will never be repaid.

Fractional-Reserve banking and government sponsored inflation work great in boom times, but at the same time they add artificially to the boom and tend to mask the economic reality.

Leverage is commonly recognized as a way to increase a force or magnify an effect by artificial means. Fractional-Reserve banking leverages one dollar into ten, twenty dollars, or even more, depending on the judgment (or lack of) shown by the bank. We have seen that it works both ways, rewarding for the bank when all goes according to plan, but with devastating losses when the borrowers can't pay back the money the bank loaned them.

Education

The golden age of Education in this United States was one hundred years ago, much of it done in one-room country schools. Unlike many other countries at the time, in the United States universal education was required, and its cost and responsibility were imposed locally. This followed Jefferson's theory that the success of a democracy depended on an informed (and educated) electorate.

The curriculum then was a no-nonsense reading, writing, and arithmetic. American and world history and geography were also covered, with some emphasis on patriotism. The first eight grades were often taught together; up to thirty children and one teacher.

Before class started in the morning, there was a Pledge of Allegiance to the flag (there was an America Flag in every room,) then the Lord's Prayer and a short reading from the Bible. After that brief opening ceremony, classes could begin.

Most of the teachers in the lower grades were young single women. Married women were not allowed to teach, and if a woman teacher did get married, she lost her job. There was not a shortage of women teachers however, because teaching was one of the few 'respectable' job opportunities open to women. So teaching was attractive to the more capable of about half of the population. What seems like unfair and discriminating rules by today's standards, had the benefit of supplying the educational system with talented teachers.

Young men were also eligible, and for many young men it was a stepping stone to better jobs. The combination of a prestigious job and the potential for advancement has always been an attractive draw for young people. A four year degree was not a requirement; there were two year 'Normal Schools' that were considered adequate training for the lower grades.

There was no 'social promotion'. If the student could not demonstrate mastery of the required grade material, he/she was held in that grade for another year. The intensity of the first eight grades was such that those completing them were well prepared and often very successful in life without further formal education.

The 'higher grades' nine through twelve were 'high school' and available but not required for all. College followed high school, and was intended for advanced specialty vocations.

When those times are compared with today's loose standards and lack of morals in the public schools, it raises doubts about the direction of the country. Many of today's parents have the same concerns and have opted for home schooling. This is commendable. There are already indications that home-schooled students are ahead of their public-schooled contemporaries. Perhaps we are witnessing the rise of a new 'golden age' in education.

A Prediction Come True

Alexis de Tocqueville in his book, 'Democracy in America,' predicted that the 'American Experiment' with democracy would fail in 200 years. He predicted that the voters would find that they could vote themselves money from the government treasury. That prediction is eerie in its accuracy.

There are now enough people, voting in blocks, who have elected federal legislators who will in turn, 'reward their friends' with money, just as predicted more than 200 years ago. (Chicago style: reward your friends and punish your enemies.) The most obvious way to stop this raid on the public coffers, is **to not allow** voters to vote in elections in which they might have a pecuniary interest. This will not be easy to do today, with so many 'entitlements' that Wasters think they deserve.

Wasters on welfare should not be able to elect officials who might give them more welfare money. Those on unemployment should not be allowed to vote for legislators who might extend or raise unemployment benefits. Such prohibitions would only be fair to the general public and especially to Producers. Wasters would be entitled only to what others in the general population considered fair and necessary.

Any recipient of federal money should not be allowed to vote in federal elections. Any recipient of state money should not be allowed to vote in state elections.

Federal bureaucrats should not be allowed to vote in national elections where they might vote for politicians who could give them higher salaries or hire more bureaucrats. State bureaucrats should not be allowed to vote in state elections where they might vote for politicians who could give them higher salaries.

The 'General Welfare' clause in the United States Constitution has been stretched far beyond its original intent, and this is becoming more obvious every day. A strict interpretation of the Constitution would be that when the 'General Welfare' clause is used to make a payment to an individual or special group, it is not 'General' it is 'Specific' and therefore is unconstitutional. To be general, any payment would have to be made identically to the whole general population. To allow only political favorites to receive benefits is unfair and unconstitutional. And to allow Wasters to influence how much they can extract from Producers, is immoral.

Ironically, the very success of the American Experiment has created such a lush and productive economy, that there are now enough Wasters to destroy it.

POLITICS AND RELIGON—and Science??

This is the part of the book I probably should not write, but the topic is so fertile with controversy, that I can't resist. So here goes.

The major religions are based on revelations from God to man. In other words, God revealed certain truths to some favored individual, physical man. But the major religions differ markedly on what was revealed. This raises the question, was God that inconsistent, or was the man side of the revelation flawed?

It reminds us of the story of the three blind men trying to describe an elephant by feeling different parts of the elephant.

The first blind man got hold of the tail, and said, "An elephant is like a rope!" His followers repeated the phrase as, "Yes, an elephant *is* a rope."

The second blind man took hold of a leg, and said, "An elephant is like a tree!" His followers repeated the phrase as, "Yes, an elephant *is* a tree."

The third blind man took hold of an ear, and said, "An elephant is like a giant leaf!" His followers repeated the phrase as, "Yes, an elephant *is* a giant leaf."

Of course the various followers disagreed on what an elephant was, and were ready to fight for what they believed in. After the three blind men were safely dead, the rope, tree, and leaf followers would each find a leader (bureaucrat) among them to tell them what to believe and to guide them.

And the elephant goes on being an elephant.

Could it be that the Greater Reality is beyond the description of mere mortals? Is our, or any vocabulary sufficient to describe the Greater Reality? Is the human intellect capable of understanding the Greater Reality? Have the translations of religious bureaucrats, through the ages, changed the original meanings of the revelations?

We have evolutionists and creationists talking past each other. Definitions are important. Can anyone tell us, how long is a day in the eyes of God? Are all days the same length? How long are six days, or seven days? If God rested on the seventh day, did He start working again? Is He still resting? Is He still working?

Could the Greater Reality be so complicated that none of the religions completely describe it? Could the Greater Reality be so large and complex that all religions correctly describe some part of it?

And the elephant goes on being an elephant.

71

Science stumbles by

In an out of print book by Hinton titled "The Fourth Dimension" he describes the perceptions of entities in different dimensions. The description was good enough for the noted scientist George Gamow to use it in his book "Adventures in Flatland."

The simplest being would be one-dimensional. It could only move on a line such as a wire or a line on paper. The entity could move back and forth along the line over time, but it would not know either right, left, up, or down. It would only know forward and backward along the line as a function of time. It could experience a flat surface, over time, by moving along a line drawn on that flat surface, but it wouldn't know if the line curved left or right.

The next step in perception would be a two-dimensional being. It could move on a flat plane and go left or right, but not up or down. It would be similar to a water bug which could move on the surface of water but not look up or down. It would only be aware of the flat surface it was floating on. However, it could experience a three-dimensional surface as a function of time. The analogy is given of fingers on a hand moving up through the surface of the water over a period of time. The two-dimensional creature could go around a finger and perceive it as an island, not knowing that the finger also existed both above and below the flat surface of the water. If the whole hand was moving up through the surface of the water, the water bug would perceive the islands as growing in size and finally merging together over a period of time, thus exposing all of the fingers as part of the hand. But the entity would not know that all the fingers were still existing above the surface of the water and part of the hand was still existing below the surface of the water.

Many animals are two dimensional in their perceptions. A friend, who was born and raised on a farm in Michigan, told me about their pet fox, which had been raised from a baby. They had to keep the fox chained up, or he would run away. The fox knew the chain was keeping him from running away, and he would cover the chain with dirt, so he couldn't see it. Then he would take a big run to get away, and he was always surprised when the chain reached up and grabbed him. He never learned. For him, if he couldn't see the chain, it did not exist.

For two dimensional beings, pockets are magic. If something is in a pocket and they can't see it, it doesn't exist. When it comes out of the pocket, and they can see it, it seems as if it appeared out of thin air. It may seem a little confusing that two dimensional beings can operate in our three-dimensional world, but they see everything as being two dimensional, even though they may have excellent depth perception. The water bug analogy is better for our concept of two-dimensional beings experiencing three dimensions as a function of time.

As human beings, we can experience three dimensions directly, as well as understand the simpler two and one dimen-sional systems. Are we now experiencing four dimensions as three dimensions over a period of time? Mystics tell us that both past and present exist, but we cannot experience them; we are stuck in a 'now' time 'wave.' Is the Greater Reality four dimensions? Five dimensions? Multiple dimensions? Is there a 'Greatest' Reality?

Theoretical physicists now tell us there are more than three dimensions, but they don't tell us where they are or how to get there. It's nice to know they found room for hell, heaven, and many mansions.

Seriously, if Earth has alien visitors from outer space, it's quite likely that they know a lot about other dimensions. Perhaps they can slide between dimensions, appear out of nowhere, and disappear again. Perhaps these other dimensions have different laws of physics, which would allow them to travel faster than the speed of light. That would be much superior to our crude chemical rockets for space travel.

Can we consciously perceive higher dimensions?

How?

"Beware of those who have more answers than questions."

The Global Warming Hoax

Meteorologists do not use science to predict the weather. They cannot write a computer program that will predict the weather, and they don't want to talk about it. Meteorologists are historians. What they do is have a computer search past weather records for conditions similar to those at the present time. They call each computer 'hit' a 'model' and then each model predicts a repeat of what happened in the past. This dates back to the Allies' Normandy landing in World War II, when that method was used successfully to predict the weather on the day of the landing. If the meteorologists cannot write a program to predict next weeks' weather, they certainly cannot predict (global) weather for years in the future.

We should look more to geologists for global changes in weather. They would tell us that there have been several 'Ice Ages' in the not too distant past, and that we are presently in a warm inter-glacial period. The past geological record is available for all to see, and is much more real than unproven theories of hoaxers and alarmists.

The scientific method would be to do a theoretical 'heat balance' of the earth and see what effect burning fossil fuels would contribute to heating the earth. Anecdotal reports say that the heating value of all the fossil fuel burned on the earth in a year is about the same as the amount of heat the earth receives from the sun in an hour. One hour is a small part of the number of hours in a year. (365 days times 24 hours per day = 8760 hours in a year.) If that is true, the heat contribution of burning fossil fuel is one part in eight thousand, seven hundred and sixty one parts of heat supplied to the earth. That is less than the variation of heat radiation from the sun attributed to sun spots.

It might be enlightening (no pun intended) to look for more sun cycles. The sunspot cycles have been observed for long enough to be reliable, but there could well be other, longer cycles. Scientists do not have a complete understanding of the sun's internal processes at this time.

Cosmologists might have some ideas on external factors such as long term repeating events from outer space or one time events that could affect the orbit of the earth and the resulting distance from the sun. If a uniform time between ice ages could be found, it would argue for a repeating celestial event.

The basic conclusion is that man-made activities are not sufficient to be a major factor in global warming. To concentrate on such a flawed theory is a misdirection of resources that could be better spent on other factors in global warming, in an effort to find the true causes.

IMMIGRATION

Pablo was an illegal immigrant working in Florida as a dishwasher. His dream was to save money and return home as a wealthy man. After eleven years, he had saved $70,000 and was ready to return to his Central America home. He would have enough money to buy a house, maybe a business or farm, and live well for the rest of his life. But federal bureaucrats caught him at the airport and confiscated his money. I haven't heard of what happened to Pablo since then, but I hope he got his money back and is living 'happily ever after' in his home country.

There are many like Pablo who would leave home, suffer even extreme inconveniences, and work at the most menial of jobs in a foreign country for some time, to get money, and then return home to live with friends and family. They don't want to live permanently in the United States, they just want to work here temporarily for more money than they could make at home. They would endure temporary inconvenience for monetary gain and future success, and then take their money and go home for the rest of their lives, living with family and friends.

One misconception that needs to be corrected is that all foreigners want to come to the United States to live permanently. Yes, there are some who would like to come here and work for the American dream, and there are others who would like to be lifetime Wasters at the expense of American Producers. But not everyone wants to live in the United States for the rest of their lives. For example, there are many Mexicans who are proud to be Mexican, and want to live in Mexico with their friends and family. That is their home. Like Pablo, they would come here to work for more money than they could get at home. And like Pablo, when they got enough money, they would take their money and go home and live well the rest of their lives.

We need a 'Guest Worker' program similar to the 'Bracero' program that was sponsored by the United States government during World War II. It would offer a chance for the 'Pablos' of the world to work here in the United States for some specified period of time. There already is a program for foreigners with 'critical' technical skills to work here, so why not have one for ordinary labor? Have 'would be' workers fill out a resume and 'would be' employers fill out a form listing the type of work desired, and then match them up. For those illegals already here, if the 'would be' employers and the 'would be' workers know each other and agree on the conditions of employment, so much the better. The new 'Braceros' could walk across the border legally and safely instead of dealing with the dangerous 'coyotes' and other smugglers.

One great appeal to the new Braceros would be that they could easily and legally return to their families for holidays and then easily and legally come back to their job in the United States, since they would 'have papers.' They could have bank accounts and drivers licenses. Those who are now here illegally might come out of hiding and sign up if they saw the advantages of the program.

The new Braceros would have to agree to certain conditions; that they were not on a path to United States Citizenship, that it was for a specified time, that they must not have criminal convictions, and that they could not bring their family across except for temporary visits. But that would be a small price to pay for being able to cross the border safely any time they wanted to. They would not have to pay thousands of dollars to some coyote or smuggler and endure the dangers of illegal crossing.

An added benefit to this program would be that all those left crossing the border illegally would be smugglers and criminals. Those who just wanted to work for a better life would not be among them. There would be little cause for sympathy for those crossing illegally. The program would have a humanitarian benefit for the new Braceros, because they would not be subject to the abuses of the smugglers and coyotes.

Those who would oppose the bracero program described here are probably those who would hold the potential new braceros hostage to their own plans for total amnesty.

They would sacrifice the safety of potential new braceros to advance their own political objectives.

Every day there are thousands of people who cross the Mexican-American border legally. If the authorities want to see a drivers license, locals show one. If they want to see a passport, locals get one to show them. Those on both sides of the border can easily obtain the 'papers' needed to cross legally, unless they are criminals. Who would cross illegally in some remote, dangerous and hard to get to place, when it is so easy to cross legally? Only those doing something illegal. We need to protect those who only want to work and better themselves by separating them from the criminals. If we had a Bracero program, we could identify all of those crossing illegally as the criminals we do not want.

The new 'Braceros' would have many benefits that they do not presently have. They might be paying more taxes, but that would be offset by being eligible for a higher wage. They would not have to accept a lower wage because they were hiding and did not want to be exposed. They could work in this country without fear of being 'exposed.'

Depopulation and Critical Mass

There are some among us who favor reducing the earth's population, some for one reason and some for another reason. The most violent and subversive of these favor the prejudiced elimination of their political critics, as practiced not long ago, in Fidel Castro's Cuba.

There is probably some practical limit to the number of people the earth can physically support, *given the level of technology at a given time.* If they don't know the level of technology, bureaucrats can't tell what the critical number of people would be. Looking back in history, we can say, yes with bare subsistence farming, the earth could only support X number of people; or with modern farming methods, it can support Y number of people. We don't want to go back to subsistence farming, nor do we know what improvements in farming may come in the future. So limiting population simply based on speculation of what the earth's 'carrying capacity' might be, is impractical speculation.

A more realistic factor, however, is the **Critical Mass of Human Endeavor.** (A new novel concept. Most readers will recognize 'Critical Mass' as being associated with an atomic bomb explosion; if a large enough mass of refined uranium is in one place, it will spontaneously explode.)

On a local level, there is a **Critical Mass of Human Endeavor**. For example, the minimum number of people in a city that will support a symphony orchestra. Actually, in this case, there are two different critical masses; one critical mass of a talent pool, to supply enough musicians, and another critical mass to supply a supporting audience. Only large cities have the needed **Critical Mass of Human Endeavor** (population) to support a symphony orchestra. There are myriad similar critical masses for numerous activities such as football stadiums, street cars, bus routes, doughnut shops, a university, a hospital, etc.

(It has been said that there are some towns too small to support one lawyer, but that there is no town so small that it can't support *two* lawyers.)

Another **Critical Mass** is based on probability statistics. The probability of having another Tesla, Edison, or Einstein, is directly related to the size of the population having children. With a small population, there is a small chance of having very many highly intelligent children growing into adults who can advance the technology.

A small population, over a longer period of time, should produce as many talented people as a larger population in a shorter time, but if you had one genius inventor and no supporting technology or other talented people, that genius would be wasted in a sea of mediocrity. This has probably happened in the past. A genius Neanderthal would be a talent sadly wasted.

Also, with a reduced population, there might not even be enough people with the needed talents to continue the existing civilization. We can look at some of the more primitive areas of the world and recognize the shortcomings of resource allocation in an isolated group of people.

When the eugenics proponents think they can beat the probability of statistics, they are showing arrogance in the expectations of their own offspring and showing their own inability to face reality.

Within limits, **The More the Merrier.**

Eugenics

In his book "The Next Hundred Years" author Furnas delivers a devastating critique of Eugenics.

He points out that eugenicists never 'look at their own blood.' They always want to change other peoples' characteristics. Of course, they assume their own kind has few flaws. (It's the family thing again, they are most comfortable with their own kind.) This brings into question, what kind of ideal people are they trying to create? And what justifications can they give for their criteria?

Geneticists tell us that it takes 30 generations to 'breed-true.' So to have the 'desired type' today, they would have had to start their breeding program at the time of the crusades. If they had started their breeding program then, using the typical crusader as their ideal, we would likely have a bunch of religious fanatics today. (Maybe it actually worked on their adversaries in the crusades, because we do have fanatic Muslims today.)

Furnas then questions how an ideal could be selected today which would be most appropriate 800+ years in the future. Without knowing what society's needs will be that far in the future, how can anyone possibly choose an ideal to work toward?

He points out that there is too much random variation in the human race to predict what the children will be. The same parents may have highly intelligent offspring and also have mental defectives, causes unknown. It would appear that a large, random variation in a species shows a great potential for adaptability to changing conditions. Prototypes are available to be tested.

Furnas goes on to point out that breeding for special properties also weakens the stock by breeding out some desirable properties. He uses silkworms as an example. They have been selectively bred for centuries to the point that they are 'incompetent insects' who cannot survive today under natural conditions, even though they are superior at producing silk.

He then gives several examples showing that an exceptional genius does not indicate that the descendants will be geniuses. One compelling example: Leonardo da Vinci's descendants are Italian peasants. The descendants of great authors, musicians, scientists, etc., are usually of normal achievement, even though they have a favorable environment.

There may be a natural diminution of mental defectives, since their lives are shorter and they are less likely to reproduce. To survive, you must be one of the fittest. (Darwin said that.)

Successful societies need a few geniuses, but where to get them? If eugenicists could achieve true-breeding, there would be no variations either above or below a general, predictable, and repeating level. It's as if getting undesirables is the price we pay for the variation that gives us geniuses.

What makes a 'genius'? It is more than mental capability. There must also be some degree of rebellion that feeds of off dissatisfaction with the conventional norm, and allows questioning of the status quo. Then there must be some curiosity into the subject that inspires investigation, followed by attempts of action, which may or may not be successful. A final requirement is persistence, hopefully resulting in an advancement for the society.

We are told that there are some species that have not changed in more than a million years. It would appear that their species has found what works best for them, and finds no need to change or adapt. If studies were made of those species, it would probably show that there is little variation in their offspring. They have 'bred-true' and now would have difficulty adapting to any change in their environment, much like the silkworm.

Endangered species today are obviously the consequence of inability to adapt to the changing circumstances of life's opportunities. Efforts to save them, while emotionally appealing, are questionable from Nature's standpoint.

Natures' Law: Adapt or Die.

Reciprocity

"What's good for the Goose is good for the Gander."

"Turnabout is fair play."

"It's payback time."

"Do unto others as you would have them do unto you."

There are historical and contemporaneous philosophical admonitions regarding Reciprocity. There is also an unwritten law among social creatures that typically says, "You leave me alone, and I'll leave you alone." Other factors may soon ensue, such as hunger, which could lead to attack for food or survival, but the neutrality concept persists for most of the time.

As a basic social phenomenon, reciprocity has many applications, from a personal to a national philosophy, and all the levels in between.

We are most familiar with reciprocity on a personal level. We drive our vehicles on the proper side of the road and expect others to do the same. We que up in a single file line for access through a door and expect others to do the same. We automatically behave in a conventional manner *and expect others to do the same.* We expect, and may even insist on, reciprocity from others.

On an international basis, much of the reciprocity is hidden from view, but distortions exist, mostly based on special interests. For instance, import taxes are grossly distorted. In essence, we are often treating other countries better than they are treating us. We let some countries ship goods into our country cheaply, while if we were to ship the same goods into their country, we would pay a heavy, prohibitive tax. Perhaps we should tax imported autos at the same rate they would tax our autos exported to their country.

Many of our 'exported jobs' are based on distortions in taxation, not just on cheaper labor. Most nations will protect their 'home producers' and maybe we should reciprocate by doing the same. Special interest groups will cry 'don't start a trade war' but fair trade should not dismissed so broadly. And don't bore us with that old 'Comparative Advantage' argument.

Immigration policies are often greatly distorted. Mexico has very severe, and strongly enforced laws against outsiders, yet Mexicans expect the United States to be lenient on Mexican nationals who may enter our country illegally. Perhaps we should change our immigration laws to match

Mexico's immigration laws. Turnabout is fair play. Similarly with other countries that put limitations on our citizens (and sometimes their own citizens) that we would not tolerate.

Religion and religious practices are notoriously different in some countries, compared to our own. It is understandable that many individuals would want to come to our country in order to practice their religion freely, but now we are seeing some who come here and want to impose their practices on us, in our own country, in violation of our laws and mores. Some even openly speak of destroying our civilization and replacing it with their own religion and laws. Worse yet, they say they will "kill non-believers." This is beyond rude and uncivilized, it is a declaration of war, culturally and physically. Reciprocity is irrelevant to them.

Religion has a broad range of allowable beliefs and practices under our Constitution, so long as the government does not specify or impose a particular religion.

(Reynolds v. U.S., 98 U.S. 145, 149.) But that does not allow unlawful acts, such as killing 'non-believers' as some 'religions' currently promise to do. Another requirement under 'Religious Freedom' also requires "the doing or forebearance of which is not inimical to the peace, good order, and morals of society." Barnette v. West Va. State Bd. Of Education, 47 F. Supp. 251, 253, 254.

In essence, the Federal Courts seem to require reciprocity of religions. All are free to practice their religion, so long as it conforms to 'peace, good order, and morals of society.' For a particular religion to claim that its own 'laws' supersede the

Constitution and our own established laws, is mockery to any claim of religious freedom.

Perhaps we need to make a distinction between religions and cults. A death cult would be more descriptive of a belief that proscribes death to others, for whatever reason.

Feelies and Thinkies

Marshall McLuhan characterized people into groups that had different cognitive approaches to life.

We will call those with an emotional approach to a subject as "Feelies." They will often start a statement with the phrase "I feel that —" because they believe their emotion is most important. (Unless they have read this.)

Those whom McLuhan called 'print' people will most often start a statement with the phrase "I think that —" because they believe they have correctly analyzed the subject, that proper analysis is most important, and will best solve a problem. We will call these 'analyzer' people "Thinkies."

We can see that when we have a person of each type debating, they will soon be 'talking past' each other. There is a tendency for Feelies to ignore the immediate reality. Their approach to environmentalism is a prime example; the Feelies have already emotionally concluded that a certain result should be achieved. Only then will they look for facts to support their conclusion. (see Conclusionary Reporting.)

The Thinkies will line up the related facts into what they think is a linear, logical manner, to prove their point.

Life is a progression of changes, internal as well as external. Children are very emotional, and they will (hopefully) move away from childish to adult reactions. It is well known that school children must 'like the teacher' to learn effectively. If they don't like the teacher, they don't learn as well. They need an emotional attachment.

Adolescence is a turbulent time for all concerned. Emotions are strong, but a new process – logic – is entering into thought processes. Hopefully, in high school, a logical maturity will set in, often taking the form of criticism and questioning of elders.

The emotional approach can be extended by exposure to liberal and artistic influences. The arts are appealing to Feelies who *feel* it expresses what *they feel*. They exult in group expressions.

Two friends can decide to go to the movies. The Feelie will have an emotional desire to go. The Thinkie will have a mental list of reasons to justify the trip. So they can go and enjoy the movie together, but each will have a different reason for attending.

Many Feelies never make the progression to cold logic; their progress is arrested in the emotional approach. They can live their life in a cozy emotional trip.

Many Thinkies progress past reality and believe everything in the world can be rationalized – or have they reached to an emotional fixation on logic ??

In old age, emotion returns and strengthens, but the attachment will likely be to different objects than in youth. The objects of emotion have changed. Nostalgia isn't what it used to be.

EPILOGUE

"The Problem, if properly analyzed, will itself, suggest a solution."

"Beware of those who have 'the solution' before they even define the problem."

We have tried to analyze parts of the government and other problems as they exist today, and give some background, yet in a popular way that can be easily understood. A full analysis would be long and tedious, and probably not a popular read.

The following 'To Do' list is similarly incomplete and not detailed. However, it is a place to start discussion.

A TO DO LIST

Have the United States Mint (or treasury) issue one ounce gold and silver coins, and make them available to only the American public at the world market price for gold and silver. (Perhaps by bid.) Let them be purchased with federal 'notes' at the market price for the metal. The prices would go up as the federal 'notes' became worth less. Eventually the federal notes would become totally worthless and irrelevant, and we would be back on a sound monetary base.

Issue gold and silver certificates instead of federal 'notes.' Tie their price to that of the gold and silver coins. Let the certificates specify how much gold or silver they represent and sell them to only Americans at the world market price.

Repeal the Civil Service system and replace it with the spoils system. This alone would make the government employees more responsible and respectful to the public. Their loyalty to their party would (hopefully) transfer over to doing a good job to show how effective their party can be.

Repeal the 'progressive' income tax, and replace it with a flat tax, with no 'deductions,' exemptions or loopholes and no 'Tax Exempt Foundations.' All income would be taxed at the same rate and there would be no 'non profit' trusts, or other organizations that were exempt from income tax. All property would be taxed by local governments. Federal land and buildings could be taxed by local governments. Same for churches, they could be taxed.

Remove or reduce the minimum wage law. There's a saying, "Bad breath is better than no breath all." Similarly, a low wage is better than no wage at all. Another big problem is unemployment insurance. Many people receiving unemployment insurance payments will not take a job that pays less than they can 'draw' on unemployment insurance (read Producers.) They could be a low level Producer, but they prefer to be a Waster receiving 'free' money.

Ban payments, loans, grants, or transfers of money between federal, state, or local governments, except for services rendered. Each level of government should be responsible for its own money coming in as taxes and expenditures going out, as it sees fit.

Establish a work pool of those drawing unemployment insurance. Let employers bid for their services, even at lower salaries than the unemployed would accept, but put them to work and let the government make up the difference to what they would be getting on unemployment insurance. It would be cheaper to the government than paying the full unemployment amount.

Make information regarding all salaries, payments or transfers of money to all elected officials and all employees of federal and state government easily available to the public. The public should know what salaries and expense money are being taken by these 'servants of the people.' This should be public information, available to all or as popularly called, Transparency.

Require all government regulations to contain the names of the bureaucrats who wrote them. Enough of the faceless, nameless bureaucrats acting behind the scenes in anonymity.

There is a perceptive statement, "It's not the fall that kills you, it's the sudden stop." So it is with changes in government policies. The 'progressives' have been using gradual change to work toward their socialist objectives, and we could employ a similar 'gradualism' to work our way back from those socialistic policies. It would make the changes easier if they were gradual instead an abrupt sudden stop.

Start with an immediate 15% reduction in federal staff and budget this year. This would be accompanied with a 10% reduction in pay at all levels. Presidential appointees would not receive any salary or supporting staff until they were approved by Congress. In succeeding years do successive percentage reductions until the budget is balanced.

Put a cap on all federal retirement payments. Make it based on the last ten years of employment retroactively, so they couldn't be boosted up in their last year to qualify for higher retirement. For those presently retired, revise their retirement to be based on the last ten years of service (?) instead of the last one or two.

Put all federal employees, retirees, and elected officials into the Social Security system instead of the present retirement system. Deduct payments from their salaries just like private workers. If they want higher retirement, let them make higher contributions or buy supplemental retirement insurance.

Eliminate federal workers health plans, except military, and put them on Medicare or Medicaid like the rest of us. If they choose, let them buy their own supplemental insurance just like the general population does.

Do not allow more than one retirement plan for government workers. Let them chose only the higher one.

Allow federal bureaucrats to be sued in state courts. Plaintiff may choose the court. Presently, federal employees will have their case 'removed' to federal courts, where their fellow federal 'bureaucrats in black robes' can help them. A state court would likely be a more level playing field.

Congress should take back responsibilities for regulations from bureaucrats, and vote its approval on all regulations on a roll call vote so voters could know how their representative voted. Pass a general 'sunset' law on all regulations by a certain future date, and then Congress would have to approve any new regulations.

Courts must judge each case on its merits, not on 'presumption of regularity' or similar trust in some bureaucrat's assertions. Bureaucrats must not be qualified as experts over testimony of others. Bureaucrats who instigate charges DO have a vested interest in the cases they bring and are NOT objective in their testimony. Government attorneys also have a vested interest in every case they bring, because their record of cases won is a badge of superior accomplishment for promotions and pay raises. Both bureaucrats and their attorneys are biased in each case they bring.

There must be a way to remove bad 'bureaucrats in black robes.' If they cannot be removed or reduced in pay, they could be reassigned to another district, where they would be considered a new appointee. If they cannot be reduced in pay, they can be held at the same pay without any increases. They might be inspired to find a way to stop the inflation that is part of the **Stealth Taxes**.

'Bureaucrats in black robes' could be required to take a one year leave of absence without pay if a popular vote in their district favored it.

Reinstate the Glass-Stegall act to separate various financial activities that might lead to collusion. Retail banks would be separate from Investment banks and Insurance companies would be separate from both and from each other.

Make it a criminal offense for a person to contribute to federal political campaigns if the person is the recipient of federal money, except for military.

Institute a new 'Bracero' program similar to the one used in World War II. Foreigners would be granted temporary status as residents, to work in this country for a specified length of time. They would not be on a path for permanent residence or citizenship, but could renew their stay if agreeable to both parties. They would have the same rights and privileges as citizens, but could not vote, hold office, or serve on juries. They could not bring in families or relatives.

Do not allow members of the bar association to be members of Congress, because they are already in the Judicial branch of the federal government.

This list is not complete or all inclusive, and its implementation is not very likely, but it's a place to start. There could be other reforms that should be done first.

Our nation's greatest threat is Arrogant, Over Paid bureaucrats. (AOP bureaucrats.) If we can correct that, it would be a great accomplishment and benefit to the nation.

The Hero I'm looking For

Politicians campaign on what they will do if elected. They will pass a law for this, they will pass a law for that, and all the good things they promise require a law.

I'm looking for the politician who will REPEAL something. We already have too many laws.

THE LOST "FRENCHY" GOLD MINE

In the early 1900s, the narrow gauge railways opened up the mountains of Colorado, and areas with mining potential that had previously been difficult to access, became relatively easy to explore. Prospectors, miners, and total greenhorns came from all over the world. The La Plata Mountains in Southwest Colorado, west of Durango, were especially accessible. The Denver and Rio Grande Railroad had a rail spur up to the mouth of the La Plata canyon, making it easy to ship ore to the smelter in Durango. There were two settlements in the La Plata Canyon, Mayday, at the mouth, and La Plata City farther up the canyon. Both 'cities' had livery stables, stores, schools, blacksmith shops, bars, pool halls and all the optimism prospectors needed. It was a busy, boisterous time and many rich discoveries were made.

One of the many world travelers attracted to the La Plata mountains was Frenchy Thomas (sp.) Not much is known about Frenchy. He was a loner, secretive, and suspicious of others, especially other prospectors and miners. But Frenchy soon had rich gold ore to show, rich tellurium ore.

Of course everyone wanted to see his mine, but Frenchy wouldn't even tell them what area it was in. Several people wanted to buy his mine, but they needed to see it first, and Frenchy wouldn't show it to them. They asked him how much he wanted for his mine, and he said, "One Million dolaire !! I go to Paree and ride the white horse !!" But no buyer would put up a million dollars without seeing the mine. So there was a standoff. Nobody would pay without seeing the mine and Frenchy wouldn't show them the mine.

It should be noted that the term 'mine' was often used loosely. It could be that Frenchy had only found a rich outcrop and never worked it enough to get underground. In that case, he probably covered it well enough that no one else would find it. Even if he did get underground, he wouldn't get very deep doing hand work alone. And there wouldn't be any dump to give away mining activity; if he wanted, he could easily carry a day's worth of tailings somewhere else and scatter them.

Olga Little, the well known lady packer in the La Plata mountains, related that when she was packing for the Gold King mine, she offered Frenchy a free ride on one of her pack animals. Frenchy declined. He was in the habit of walking wherever he went. He didn't have a horse or pack animals of his own, he carried everything on his back. This suited him fine for prospecting. He could go anywhere he could climb, and there are plenty of challenging mountains to climb in the La Platas, where that is the only way to prospect.

Some people tried to follow Frenchy, to find out where his mine was, without success. However, it was common knowledge that Frenchy's mine was near Eagle Pass, at the head of Lewis Creek.

Eagle Pass is a beautiful, broad, grassy area at the head of Lewis Creek. A jeep trail goes through it to the Western Belle mine. It is a great place to picnic, and locals often made a day of it there. The views are spectacular. To the west, the mountains on the west side of the La Platas are clear and sharp. To the east, you look over the top of Durango and see the southern mountains of the San Juan system and the 'Pyramid' north of Pagosa Springs. To the north is Lewis Mountain and a trail to the Western Belle. To the south, on a gradual and long trek is Baker Peak and an old trail to the Jenny Lind mine.

Looking to the east from Eagle Pass, it's obvious why Frenchy choose the Gold King trail to get to his mine. Some tributaries of Lightner Creek head on the east side of Eagle Pass, but the topography is steep. There are not many good trails up Lightner Creek. And even now, we don't know if Frenchy's mine was on the east side of the ridge or west side. Often times, the best access is an indirect route, and his mine could just as well be on the west side of the ridge, past the Jenny Lind.

Frenchy would go up the Gold King trail, past the Ashland-Tenbroeck mine to Eagle Pass. From there, only Frenchy knew where to go. In that area there were well known rich mines operating, such as the Western Belle, Durango Boy, Durango Girl, and the Jenny Lind. Frenchy's ore was similar, but experts on those mines agreed that Frenchy's ore did not come from them. His ore was from somewhere else.

There are reasons other than paranoia for Frenchy not wanting others to know the location of his 'mine.' At the time he was showing his 'ore' there were claims plastered all over the vicinity of Eagle Pass. It could be that he knew what he had found was on somebody else's claim, and if they knew, they would claim it, as they were entitled to. If he staked a claim on it, even though it was a new find, it could lead to litigation.

Also, in nearby Puzzle Pass, there was a character we'll call Mr. 'Intimidation' who always carried two 'six-guns.' Mr. Intimidation and his several sons, had what could only be called 'traveling claims.' When anyone staked a claim in that area, Mr. Intimidation and his sons would visit them and explain that the area had already been staked and they had better get off of his claim. Mr. Intimidation and his sons tended to be effective in discouraging other prospectors from working in 'his' area.

Working alone, Frenchy never shipped any ore. Even a rich mine requires equipment, supplies, and miners. To develop it, Frenchy would need help, and any activity would be noted by others, and Frenchy didn't want to give away the location. Surely Frenchy had to know about staking mining claims, but he was so suspicious that he wouldn't stake it, because that would tell everyone where it was. So

Frenchy never showed his mine to anyone and never sold it to anyone, and Frenchy never went to Paree and never rode the white horse.

Henri Tomas, a frenchman, died a pauper on January 14, 1932. He was buried in Block 18 of Greenmount Cemetery in Durango, Colorado.

ODE TO CECIL

After the Civil War, there was a major migration of enthusiastic young men to the western United States. Extension of the railroads offered the means, and the mineral wealth of the mountain states offered the incentive for exploration. Additionally, the invention of dynamite greatly increased the productivity of miners. Mining has always been dangerous, and the use of dynamite didn't change that. There was a crucial need for experienced miners, who could use the new technology and achieve greater production than before. Mine operators would willingly pay a premium wage for a skilled miner.

Enter the 'tramp' miner. Tramp miners were capable, confident and experienced in their craft. They could come in, take over the mining operation, and increase productivity significantly. Mine owners and operators were glad to see them come, and later, often glad to see them go. They were hard-working, competent, and often inspired increased productivity from other workers. After a hard days work in the mine, at night they would hit the bars, where they would drink and fight, and they excelled at both.

Cecil was a late comer to the tramp miner tradition. Handwork, such as single jacking and double jacking with drill steel, had been replaced by the column drill. The Jackleg (or air leg) drill had replaced the column drill, and that was Cecil's specialty. The modern jackleg drill provided maneuverability, speed, and avoided the dreaded silicosis of early steam and air rock drills. (Water fed down the center of the drill steel makes harmless mud of the powder-like cuttings.) The drill holes had to be in the proper pattern to break the rock to the right size for mucking out. Cecil had mined hard rock and soft rock and could adjust the hole pattern accordingly. He knew what and how much explosive to place in each hole for best results.

Although age was taking its toll, Cecil still had the cocky attitude and confidence that he could always 'rustle' a job wherever he happened to be. But times had changed. Big companies had taken over the big mines, the smaller mines had largely been worked out, and the total number of active mines was much smaller. The glory days of the tramp miner were coming to an end. Mining methods had also changed. Underground mining with adits, drifts, stopes, and contract work had given way to large open-pit mines. The big producers didn't have underground workings as in the past. Hard rock miners like Cecil, had fewer places to work. There were still underground mines, but the supply of miners was such that operators preferred steady workers who would settle down in the area of the mine, raise families, and be part of the community. They would not have to pay a premium for tramp miners when they could have cheaper, steady help.

Cecil enjoyed traveling to different mining areas, talking to the old-timers, new-timers, and anyone associated with mines, rocks, and minerals. Over the years, Cecil had acquired some 'high-grade' and other rock samples, which he could trade and eke out a living. He could pick up specimens that were common in one area and sell them for a profit in another area, or at a rock show. Giving a common specimen a new fancy name would often let the buyer think he had purchased a rare find. Cecil was also on the lookout for seasonal work, when people would be doing assessment work on their mining claims. So it was he met Glen, who was running a drift in his mining claim for the annual assessment work.

Glen was a seasonal miner. He had inherited the family mining claims, and continued working them more out of familial responsibility than passion. He had seen all aspects of mining but had little experience 'doing it.' He was quite willing to have someone else drill and shoot a round for him. Mucking out the round could be done in a more leisurely fashion. So Cecil and Glen made a deal that appeared to be to the liking of both.

On an agreed upon morning, not too bright and early, Glen got the compressor up and running, the jackleg drill carried to the back of the drift, and they were all ready to drill when Cecil arrived.

Cecil had his mining attire, hard hat with headlamp, waterproof work gloves that didn't match, and steel-toed boots. His belt went through only one loop of his battery, so the battery hung askance at an angle. He didn't look professional, but his confidence shone through. Rheumy eyes that had seen better days, looked at the world with optimism and confidence. Cecil was ready.

"You got any earplugs?" he asked Glen.

"No" answered Glen.

"I figgered as much"

Cecil then reached into his shirt pocket and pulled out two filters from cigarettes he had smoked. He proceeded to stuff one in each ear and then with a fresh one lit and in his mouth, he was ready to drill holes.

As they walked to the back of the drift, Glen wondered how long the cigarette would stay lit when the drilling started and the return water blew out of the hole.

At the back, Cecil surveyed the face and decided to put a five-hole burn in the center. He'd start with a four foot steel and then deepen all the holes later with a six foot steel. That was about all you could pull in a five-by-seven drift. A five-by-seven drift. A piece of cake, probably less than twenty holes, even with four lifters.

Cecil explained to Glen where he wanted the holes. Glen would be the chuck-tender and hold the turning drill steel to start the hole, and then get out of the way so Cecil could give the drill full throttle.

The first hole went exactly as planned. Cecil then put a tamping stick in it so he could get the angle right on the other holes. Glen was glad he wore his 'diggers' (bright yellow rain gear) or he would have been soaked with the water squirting out of the bit when starting each hole. Glen wondered why Cecil didn't cut off the water until the bit was a few inches in the face, but it did prevent dust.

The rest of the holes went as planned, even the four lifters. Cecil started them at a sharp angle for the first inch or two and then had Glen bring up the mucker to put the jackleg against the bucket. Then he laid the drill and leg flat on the floor, so the lifters would be almost horizontal.

With the holes all drilled to four feet, Cecil changed to the six-foot steel and was ready to deepen all to six feet. But first he had to have a cigarette. Then they went into the powder magazine and made up primers with timed delays, so the holes would fire in a sequence that would 'pull' the burn first, then relievers, trimmers, and finally the four lifters.

Returning to the face, Cecil started at the top, deepening each hole. But the drill seemed heavier. Cecil could tell he was tired, probably because he was out of shape—he hadn't been drilling many holes lately, but he could still do it. He'd soon get his money from Glen and be down the road.

Halfway through deepening the holes, Cecil noticed his stomach was upset. Not surprising, the booze he had last night didn't like working for a living. Then he got a painful cramp in his arm. Not the right time to get another cramp when he was almost finished, but then his leg buckled and he fell down beside the drill, which was still on. With his weight off the drill, the jackleg pushed up, binding the drill steel against the side of the hole, and stalled the drill.

Cecil blacked out, but momentarily came to. He was lying down on the floor, and his right side was wet and cold. HE WAS IN THE PISS DITCH !!! How embarrassing and disgusting. Cecil was humiliated, and then passed out again.

Glen saw what happened. Cecil had been alright one minute, but then suddenly fell down. Glen turned the drill off and rushed to Cecil's side. Cecil did not respond when Glen rolled him over on his back. This was not good. Glen dragged Cecil to the mucker bucket, and rolled him into it. Then he started the mucker and backed it out of the drift.

After calling the emergency number for an ambulance, Glen again tried to revive Cecil. It was no use. When the ambulance arrived, the crew immediately tried to revive Cecil, without success. After they left, Glen felt a great sadness. He was alone now, and the compressor was still running, as if nothing had happened. Glen drove the mucker back down the drift to where they had been working just a short time ago. The drill was still in the hole Cecil had been deepening. Glen turned the drill on, and it responded with the same deafening roar, as it always had.

Glen finished deepening the rest of the holes. He loaded the drill in the bucket and backed the mucker out of the drift. Then he went into the powder magazine and got the primers Cecil had prepared. Back at the face, Glen pushed in the primers in the proper order, short delays in the burn, longer delays in holes farther from the burn, and the four longest delays in the lifters, at the bottom. Put in some anfo, then some stemming, and the primer's wires could be tied together and to the shot wire. The round was ready to fire.

Glen checked everything at the face. Wires were all tight. Tools and equipment were moved down the drift far enough to not be hit by rocks from the blast. He went back to the mucker and took the shotwires over to the battery.

As he looked back down the drift, he knew that there in the darkness, Cecil's work was about to be culminated. In a soft voice, as he touched the shotwires to the battery he said, "Here's to ya, Cecil."

The instant shaking under his feet told Glen the blast had started, then the sound came down the drift in distinct 'booms.' He counted them and concluded that all had fired.

Glen walked out of the drift, into the bright sunlight, and turned off the compressor. He would come back tomorrow when the dynamite smoke had cleared, and see how Cecil's round had pulled.

TREES

I think that I shall never face
A tree as lovely as a parking space.

An open space whose wideness beckons,
To new and old and even wrecked ones.

A space that's open, long and wide,
My little car would fit inside—of.

I'm not alone in this desperate endeavor,
Other cars are circling, it seems forever.

I see a space there, I must not linger,
Dang, she cut me off, and waved her finger.

Poems are made by fools and others,
I'd stay at home if I had my Druthers.